First Nations Women's Writings
A Study in Gender, Colour and Race

First Nations Women's Writings
A Study in Gender, Colour and Race

MERLIN KARRA

Prestige Books International
New Delhi

Published by
Prestige Books International
New Delhi 110 060
prestigebooks@gmail.com
Phone: 9818755529

Associate Office
P.O. Box 2250
Sydney 2001
Australia

ISBN: 978-81-956029-8-8

Printed in India

Contents

Preface

Canada is well known for cultural fusion. Multiculturalism is not only the government policy but also the given reality. One could see the flowering of the British, French and American cultures. The latest to flower and assert is the Native Culture. Each group has been producing its literature and has been busy asserting and preserving its identity. Amongst the Native writers, a separate small canon of the women Native writers exists whose writings are a blatant critique of mainstream White Canada. Long unheard, often brutally silenced, and more often than not spoken for by white Canadians, Canadian Native women are increasingly correcting the misdefinitions and defining themselves, writing their own stories. In doing so, they provide an indication of potential directions towards a world in which oppression on the basis of sex, race, or class does not have to be a given. Native Canadian women writers can only provide these indications of hope for the future from a particular place in time and understanding. This place is near the end, or the beginning of the end, of an examination of the forces of oppression. As Native women writers locate the roots of their oppression on the basis of race, sex and class in Canada's colonial history, they also begin to find the means of changing the system which perpetuates that oppression.

Some of the consequences of sexism, racism, and classism for Native women in Canadian society are documented in books like Maria Campbell's *Halfbreed* (1973) and Beatrice Culleton's *April Raintree* (1983) which illustrate the truth of Lee Maracle's assertion in *I Am Woman* (1988) that, like sexism, 'racism is for us, not an ideology in the abstract, but a very real and practical part of our lives' (2). Jeannette Armstrong in *Slash* (1985) provides a more thorough and complex description and analysis of racism, sexism and classism as the by-products of colonialism. The book focuses on Canadian First Nations literature and studies the output of the postcolonial writers as writings, as they resist the imposition of the European genre distinctions.

The book examines the distortions done to the image of the Canadian First Nations, and brings to light the First Nations writer's attempts to recuperate their lost status through their writings. The book examines four major ethnic writers of the Native Canadian world, Maria Campbell (b. 1940), Jeannette Armstrong (b. 1948), Beatrice Culleton (b. 1949) and Lee Maracle (b. 1950), who took up the task of challenging female subjugation. The works of these writers stood as testimonies to illustrate the truth of native women's assertion in confronting sexism and racism. These writers make literary textuality a tool in their hands to express themselves and articulate the political and social issues affecting the Natives.

Maria Campbell is one of Canada's most popular Metis authors. She was born in Park Valley, Saskatchewan, in 1940 to parents of Scottish, Indian and French descent. Her works have provided a voice to the Metis people and enabled them to be understood. She grew up in a Road Allowance community near Prince Albert National Park. Campbell has a strong sense of history. She inserts the narrative so forcibly and repeatedly into history that the reader cannot but read the play as a slice from a centuries-long struggle. Campbell belongs to Metis race, mixed blood people halfbreed, neither White nor Native but a race born out of the Native and White parents. Incidentally her autobiography is titled *Halfbreed* (1973). She has focused on issues pertaining to Metis history. Campbell started to write as a means to healing her own self. *Halfbreed*, her best-selling autobiographical novel, begins with a letter to herself. The novel proved to be only the beginning of her creative endeavours. She starts with a quick overview of the history and situation of the halfbreeds in Saskatchewan, which seems to have been a happy one, up until the age of fifteen. Campbell was only in her early thirties when her book was published. Her writing is dense. She unflinchingly sets down the hatred, the social, political and economic inequities that led to the downward spiral of her own life after a disastrous marriage at fifteen. She spares herself nothing. No one has spoken more precisely, more evocatively, of what mixed-blood people, especially women, have faced.

Her book is quite unlike any other. The stories were not 'collected.' They are not taken from any old-time story-hunter's gatherings. They belong to real people, and have reality as told. There is truth in every word. *Halfbreed* recounts the first 33 years of her life and tells how Maria lost her mother when she was only 12 years old, leaving her to look after her younger siblings. In an effort to keep her family together, young Maria married an abusive white man who reported her to child welfare authorities and her siblings were placed in foster homes. Devastated, Maria moved to Vancouver where her husband deserted her; subsequently, she turned to a life of drugs and prostitution. Alone and desperate, she attempted suicide twice and was hospitalized. It is in the hospital that Maria joined Alcoholics Anonymous and began a journey of healing.

In the novel, Maria not only tells her own story but also speaks of the discrimination and racism that affect all Metis people. In the introduction, she says, 'I write this for all of you, to tell you what it is like to be a half-breed woman in this country. I want to tell you about the joys and sorrows, the oppressing poverty, the frustrations and the dreams' (8). Although Maria's story is one of stress and crisis, it is also a story of courage and resilience. She is no longer a scared little girl but a strong independent woman full of hope for herself and her people. *Halfbreed* is a story of survival, of overcoming a sense of shame related to ethnic identity. Campbell brings attention to the way in which race in the Canadian multicultural society has been seen as real and definable. She describes the consequences of such racial thinking on Metís individuals (half-breeds or non-status Natives), the humiliating situations Métis or Native people have experienced in their everyday lives and the consequent, debilitating sense of shame shared by many of them. She continues to write and is considered an important voice in Native and feminist literary circles.

Another accomplished writer who illustrated the truth of native women's assertion is Jeannette Armstrong. She is an impassioned Indigenous rights activist who is concerned with land rights and democratic rights and improving the Aboriginal education system. Armstrong's main goal in writing is to educate young people about Native culture and history. Among her many literary works, perhaps the best known is *Slash* which is considered as the first novel by a First Nations woman in Canada. Armstrong stands as Canada's most active, determined and diligent promoter of First Nations literature and of cultural and political self-determination.

Beatrice Culleton Mosionier is another Canadian métis author, who is most notable for her novel *In Search of April Raintree.* The novel is also autobiographical; unlike Campbell, Culleton wrote for herself. Her book served as a catharsis so that she could finally come to terms with her personal history. The story included traumatic incidents from her own family life, including the suicide of two of her sisters and her own experience of being raped. A revised edition of *In Search of April Raintree* was published in 1984 with the title *April Raintree*. The main difference between the two is that *April Raintree* contains a more graphic rape scene. Mosionier's second novel, published in 2000, is titled *In a Shadow of Evil*. It is set in the Canadian Rockies and follows the life of a young girl going through family trauma and foster care. The novel was inspired by Mosionier's molestation by a priest at the age of three.

Another popular Canadian First Nations poet and author is Lee Maracle. Maracle is one of the most prolific aboriginal authors in Canada and a recognized authority on issues pertaining to aboriginal people and aboriginal literature. She is an award-winning poet, novelist, performance storyteller, scriptwriter, actor and keeper/ mythmaker among the Stó:lō people. 'The voices of the UNHEARD cannot help but be of value,' states Lee Maracle on the first page of *I Am Woman*: reality is more accurately perceived from the bottom of a hierarchical society than it is from the top. The novel is the story of one woman's search for the truth. It addresses the Native people in desperate circumstances, who need to recover the broken threads of their lives.

The first chapter of the present examines the manifestations of imperialism on the lives of First Nations women from feminist perspective. It is found that even in the colonial world, First Nations people lived in a subordinate position, the phallocentric cultural background of the colonialists placed the men in a slightly superior position. Hence an exegesis of the attempts of the female writers to interrogate and destabilize the double subjugating tactics on them through their writings is given.

The second chapter contextualizes with the support of post-colonial theories how First Nations writers 'write back' resisting the falsifications. They explicate the Europeans' pursuance of their agenda of subjugation of the First Nations people by denying their history, inferiorizing their culture, stifling their language and imposing negative images on them. First Nations writings are attempts to reclaim their heretofore suppressed history, culture, language and image and to assert their identity, dismantling the discursive hegemony of the Europeans. Though lasciviousness is imposed as part of the image of the First Nations, Natasha asserts that it is an attribute of the European settlers and explorers. She contends for this alternative vision by pointing out that the Europeans fantasized that in the orient, there is no social constraint on their strange sexual excesses.

This stimulus is reflected in the writings of the early traders and explorers. In the name of Christianizing and civilizing the African First Nations, the Missionaries exploited them. Reverent A.W. Banfield's photograph of a young African woman and his exegesis of it tell implicitly his exploitation of the woman. She is the symbol of the nameless hunted animal and he is the hunter with the camera attempting to fix her into static space.

The third chapter deals with the recuperation of the cultural practices and downplaying of imperial master narratives, resistance to falsification of history and suppression of language, a tendency reflected globally in the stage performances. Nostalgia for the lost biocentric and eco-friendly culture reflected in poetry and plays of First Nations writers is discussed. The resistance to falsification of First Nations image as part of the decolonizing project is also contextualized in this chapter.

The fourth chapter begins with the argument that the imperialists had falsified the history, culture and image of the peoples of the colonized lands to justify their presence in the land of indigenous peoples. A survey on the falsifications is necessitated, as it is part of the process of the reclamation of the lost status of the First Nations. The chapter ends with the thematic illustrations of Maria Campbell's *Halfbreed* and Beatrice Culleton's *In Search of April Raintree*.

The fifth chapter examines history and theory of Indigenous feminism, followed by the effects of colonization. It examines the issues of marginalization of Aboriginal women in Canada, Indian Act Gendered Discrimination and ends with confronting violence against Indigenous women. The book concludes by assessing the present-day predicament of First Nations people in general and women in particular and surveying the manifestations of neo-imperialism in contemporary life.

The Discourse of First Nations Women

> The dictates of patriarchy demand that beneath the Native male comes the Native female. The dictates of racism are the native men and beneath white women and Native females are not fit to be referred to as women. (Lee Maracle, *I Am Woman*, 18)

As resistance writings have the specific political agenda of dismantling the hegemonic boundaries and determinants of imperialism, it is interrelated with feminist and class-based discourses. Consequent to colonialism, female status in postcolonial societies denigrated considerably forcing them to remain a different sect, which they themselves demarcate as a fourth world group. They had been socially and spatially discriminated, as the First Nations feminist writer Lee Maracle observes, the gender stratification posits First Nation women as a doubly marginalized group (*I Am Woman* 18).

A close examination of the history of the various tribes of pre-colonial Canada brings to light how colonialism's parameters of hegemonic masculinity and heterosexuality have gradually consigned women to positions of subordination and anonymity.

Unlike in European societies, women enjoyed positions of centrality in the Indian communities. Men's absence for long periods as they went for hunting and fighting necessitated women's assuming greater responsibility in supporting the family and the clan. They were ancillary to hunting and gathering and craft production, which engendered their wielding a crucial role in the economies that developed around fishery and farming. Though labour was divided on gender basis, women laboured hard in supporting the family.

Unlike in the Christian marriages, women in the pre-colonial societies enjoyed autonomy in conjugal relationships, which dismissed the question of any feminist movement in the pre-colonial Indian societies. However, the lives of women appeared to be drudgery to the outside view consequent to the failure to realize the status and social power the women assumed through their equal participation in the economy. The assumption of patriarchal ownership and control of the economy and the male-dominated hierarchical system of the Europeans began to empower men and the First Nations women were disempowered from their roles as advisors and respected Elders of the society. The fur trade involved interaction between the two entirely different racial groups. The European traders were all male which suggested that Indian women could play a significant role in the fur trade. Thus, in the initial stages of contact, First Nations wives had been offered to the European traders in order to cement their relations through family ties and such marriages maintained an egalitarian reciprocity between the friends of both parties (Bishop 40).

Charles Mackenzie, the European writer, points out that the traders exploited certain customs prevalent among some Indian tribes, along with the sexual freedom of the First Nations. In the buffalo calling ceremony among the Mandan tribe, there existed a strange practice. Elder men with supernatural powers transmitted their powers to young men. For this, young wives of these men had sexual relations with such older men so that they in turn could transmit their power to their husbands. The Indians regarded the white man's remedies for physical ailments superior to their own and considered them equal to their shamans. They began inviting the white man for their ceremonies. Women also became interested in white men as sources of supernatural power. (448-49).

The differential treatment accorded to women was coterminous with the patriarchal orientation. The legal structures of Europe are rooted in this male dominating ideology and the denial of the conjugal rights First Nations women enjoyed in their migratory band was consequent to this ideology. The European program of projecting the First Nations women as negative entities in colonial discourse, often conflated with nature, animals and the exotic gathered momentum, and the patriarchal assumptions consigned First Nations women to positions of anonymity.

It had not been loose morality on the part of the Indians to form marital alliance with the Europeans. But the European traders failed to recognize the Indian spirit behind these marriages and they often took it as a 'marriage for convenience.' To many of them these relationships were of a fleeting nature and when they returned to Europe it was their prerogative either to turn off their defeathered women to their First Nations communities or to hand them over to other Europeans.

Though in the early stages such women and their children were welcomed, they became unwelcome in the First Nations communities gradually, because of the changing social and economic conditions. Such redundant wives found themselves between two worlds—neither white nor First Nations. In the absence of a better choice, many of them drifted into prostitution, a practice that was unheard of in First Nations societies.

Reductionist tendencies were affected in interracial marriage by the arrival of European wives and the influence of missionaries. The European Government's fear of miscegenation runs through the encouragement of the coming of European women who were projected as the harbingers of culture and civilization to the 'savages.' The Northwest Company's ruling in 1806 prohibiting its employees taking First Nations wives points at this attitude of the whites. Ethnic prejudice and authoritarian disposition acted as causation of traders' differential treatment of First Nations women. In well-established trade centres interracial marriages soon lost its relevance and voyagers even began to take advantage of their superior position by forcefully seizing First Nations women and selling them to men for money. This incurred the hostility of Indians and violent incidents like the Henley House Massacre in 1755 were the results of violation of Indian sensibilities (Bishop 39).

Impositions of European culture meant dwindling options and opportunities for First Nations women. The ready-made trade goods from Europe threatened the crafts of women, which in turn undercut their hold on society. The phallocentric English common Law denied any autonomy to women. Access to ownership of property, an essential element for independence was also disallowed. Husbands even enjoyed the right to punish wives. By European gender stratification the powers traditionally enjoyed by women were taken away and granted to men. Until 1951, women were denied the right to hold any elected office or to partake in band meetings.

European methods of data collection and interpretation of First Nations life were mostly inaccurate with their ingrained racial biases. When a Cree Chief complained to the Prime Minister how due to destitution First Nations women were compelled to 'commodify their sexuality,' the officials dismissed the reason and attributed it to the inherent lasciviousness of First Nations women. Instead of finding out the causation, disciplinary measures were enforced by adding a provision in the Indian Act to easily convict First Nations women for prostitution (*Edmonton Bulletin* 1883). Maintenance of separate criminal legislation reveals the discrimination and deep-rooted racial prejudice in the Canadian society (Backhouse 420-22).

The Causation of the introduction of the pass system for First Nations women to approach European settlements is the racial prejudice along with the European assumption that they are motivated by immoral purposes. Any woman seen in the vicinity of the town without a pass would be ordered out immediately. *The Saskatoon Herald* (15 March 1886) reported many incidents of the Northwest Mounted police cutting off locks of hair of women, who refused to leave the town at the behest of the police. By curtailing their freedom of movement, First Nations women were obstructed from finding a market for their artifacts in town, a traditional means of survival. Further, the pass system denied them certain requirements like medical services. As Tiffin, Griffiths and Ashcroft maintain "Women . . . have been relegated to the 'other' marginalized and in a metaphorical sense, 'colonized.' They had 'no space from where' they can 'speak'" (*Empire Writes Back* 174, 177).

Women were in particular portrayed as a hindrance to progress by whites. One inspector of Indian Agencies once reported that women are a hindrance to the advancement of the First Nations community, feeling that they don't allow their men to save money for better purposes. They lavish it on visiting their relatives or by giving feasts (Voyageur 110). Such coding was there because the whites view the First Nations life through their cultural perspective and undermine the First Nations commitment to culture and community.

Because of poverty in the Reserves many people lived together in shacks built of mud and hay. Such houses could not have a neat and tidy look. Instead of appreciating their adaptability, First Nations women were blamed for uncleanliness and poor housekeeping. Again, women were blamed for the high mortality rate of infants and the unhealthy conditions of the reserves.

The images of women were dichotomized. First Nations women were portrayed as agents of immorality and menace to cultured society, while European women were the harbingers of culture and civilized life. The elevated image attributed to white women is reflected in the writings of Mrs. George Cran. To her, the European woman is the embodiment of refinement, culture and endurance. To the whites, she is definitely better equipped to occupy the land, with her courage and good reason 'than the ignorant often lazy, often slovenly lower class [First Nations] women' (109).

First Nations writer Paula Gunn Allen observes that the subjugation of women was effected even in the spirit world. Many female deities were replaced by male deities. Hopi Goddess Spiderwoman was replaced by Tawa. The Cherokes deity River Foam was replaced by Thunder and the Iroquois goddess Sky Women's disempowerment is affected as she is presented as receiving her divinity from her dead father (41).

The double marginalization of women is a universal phenomenon in the colonial societies. Black American writer Toni Morrison explicates this experience in the American societies. In *Song of Solomon* (1977), the female characters speak out about the exploitation of them by men. Sethe in *Beloved* (1987) experiences her disadvantageous position as a woman at the hands of her slave master.

Beatrice Culleton observes that these stereotypes are constructed by the Europeans for their own advantage. The two assailants who rape the protagonist in her novel *April Raintree* define their victim's identity in terms of racial and sexual promiscuity. They call her a 'squaw' and 'savage' (111-14). Government, mainstream society and at times their own men place the First Nations women in a satiation of 'multiple Jeopardy.' As First Nations, Indians are discriminated against and the Indian women are doubly discriminated against (Gerber 69, 72).

Since the operational structures of the colonial government are controlled by patriarchy, women's position continued to denigrate. They resorted gender as a ploy for the imposition of patriarchal hegemony on women and the denial of their rights and sexual harassments. The Europeans enacted laws—Indians Acts—that defined and discriminated against Indians in terms of gender. A court ruling in 1866 invalidated First Nations women's rights to their white husband's property. Their offsprings also were not entitled to any share. The first act that officially discriminated against women was the Indian act 1869, section 12 (1) b that deprived an Indian woman of her status when she married a non-Indian. A farm wife had no right to own land or any legal claim on family property. Her husband had the right to ownership. He can dispose of it at his will. Sometimes even dower rights were guaranteed to the widow, on her willingness to remain as a widow. Such gender biased provisions subordinated women, thus contributing to cultural changes in the Indian communities, which had previously acknowledged the centrality of women. They were denied access to jobs and positions of influence. An Indian and northern affairs study shows that Indian women were in worse economic situations than Indian men and non-Indian women. They form 26% of the Indian labour force as against the 43% for non-Indian women. Indian women's life expectancy was two years less than that of non-Indian women. According to A Demographic Profile of the Department of Indian Affairs, Indian women are the 'the most severely disadvantaged groups in the Canadian society' (31).

The ancillary role attributed to women in the sexiest society is reflected in Jeannette Armstrong's *Slash*. The advantages of the patriarchal culture are exploited by even Slash, the protagonist, who is an activist of the Indian movement. Women are commodified and marginalized by many of the Indian leaders as Slash observes, 'there are always chicks [women] around to help with making food and things' (77). While the activists were on the move along with a comfortable stay and food, they have the opportunity to have 'chicks for company' (108). Even as they fight the racism and classism of the colonial society, the men exploit the sexism of the society.

Though Canada guarantees equal opportunities of education to women, they have to overcome many barriers to enjoy this privilege. The pressures of nuclear family and single-family systems keep women away from educational institutions. Women who aspire for higher learning are often forced to choose between learning and family. Often they are pressurized to take up the more respected role of the mother. The imposition of the traditional roles is an inhibiting factor to ambitious women.

Men's unwillingness to loosen their grasp on the power attributed to them by the colonial government is one reason for women's present predicament. The polemics of patriarchy compelled women to migrate to urban centres to eke out a living.

Employing away from home was propelled by the advent of industrialization. Women stepped into this field by helping their husbands to support the family. Gradually women tried to be self-employed and balance the family responsibility. Reserve women began experiencing the discrimination with respect to race and gender. When they applied for jobs, male chauvinism and racial and sexual prejudices came to the fore with the white employers. They were given jobs that the white and First Nations men would not do, such as mean manual labour. But their problems in this field were largely ignored by the government or institutions of employment, due to the unequal power relations of gender and race.

At home, in issues like family violence, men were usually the perpetrators, women and children were the victims. But such issues won't be propped up by men as a social problem. Collective experiences of oppression and discrimination propelled women's urge to create a female fraternity to articulate their needs and to fight against oppression. When women began organizing themselves, it resulted in a polemic with their own men. The women who dared to voice their rights were branded as trouble-makers and were isolated in the society. Such regressive action accelerated the formation of women's unions that took firm forward steps.

Feminist activists began with 'Social Feminism' aimed at improving the condition and role of women at home. They argued for added social roles for women to the degree of voicing for their right to self-determination and equality which led to the petitioning for the rights to the government, pointing out the gradual submissive measures undertaken by the government in collusion with the patriarchal systems. But the feminist movement which gathered momentum in the 1960s was largely propelled by white middle-class women. Due to its myopic concept, its recommendations excluded the issues of First Nations women or other visible minority women. Despite their commonalities, it failed to homogenize issues and demands, owing to their racial and cultural orientations, which drove First Nations women to conditions of invisibility.

Since the women's movement succeeded in changing the condition of White mainstream women, it generally came to be treated as a white women's movement. As the African American editor, Susan Mc Henry says: 'if you start talking about the women's movement, you hear a lot about what we believe and what white women believe' (qtd. Kaminer 3). Since First Nations women share the feeling that White Women's movement has nothing to do with the problems faced by First Nations women, they resisted any alignment with the feminist movement initiated by white women.

Multiplicity of significant factors contributed to this. Though feminism originated as a reaction to exclusion, its social and political agendas are truncated by exclusiveness. White women never bothered about the participation of First Nations women and the First Nations women lacked knowledge of the feminist movement, in its initial stages. Though there are commonalities in the grassroots issues like female gender oppression, when they deserve equal rights regional diversities and geographic distance make a generalizing of the feminist movement difficult. White women often failed to recognize First Nations women's concerns and their consequent consciousness of the polarities existing between the worlds of the white women and their own, and racism of the whites added to the First Nations women's feeling of exclusion from the white community. The historical, cultural and geographic grounding of the First Nations women does not allow them to count themselves with the European women as a homogeneous group.

White feminist reluctance to relinquish their racial privileges prevented the possibility of any equation between the situations of the two. Brooks observes: 'White feminist scholars pay hardly more than lip service to race as they continue to analyze their own experiences in the ever more sophisticated forms.' (252)

The First Nations women's perception of the racist orientation of white women and their hegemonic attitude make them apprehensive of their motives and alienate them from the mainstream feminist movement. Valerie Amos and Pratibha Parmer even suggest that the objectification of Third world women in European feminist discourses needs to be challenged (Mongia 177). C.T. Mohanty maintains, 'Western feminists alone become the true subjects of the counter history. Third world women on the other hand never rise above the debilitating generality of their subject status' (71).

The realization that there exists variations in the terrains of West feminism and Third world feminism makes Sara Suleri clarify the 'us' versus 'them' stand: "The moment demands urgent consideration of how the outsidedness of cultural criticism is being translated into that most tedious dichotomy that puts the 'academy' against the real world. While I am somewhat embarrassed by the prospect of having to contemplate such a simplistic binarism, this essay seeks to question its own cultural parameters by situating both its knowledge and its ignorance in relation to the devastating rhetoric of 'us' and 'them' that beleaguers issue of identity formation today" (756).

Though white women enjoyed an empowered position in the colonial societies, as they were in complicity with colonialism, the white phallocentric systems place them in a complicated space. Hence there had been disunity in the attribution of priorities. When the white women were struggling for self-fulfillment, the First Nations women were struggling for survival, for the basic necessities of life. When white feminism challenges patriarchy's subordination of women, the first Nations women's movement challenges the marginalization of first Nations woman effected in the society by the imposition of white codes and more under colonialism, in a society that had been gynocritic. White feminists are ignorant of the fact that gynarchial societies had existed in the Americas among the first Nations. Lee Maracle voices the discrepancy in the first Nations women's joining hands with the white women in the women's movement. To her the feminist movement is 'not all-inclusive.' She clearly redefines the first Nations women's issues, "I am not interested in gaining entry to the doors of the 'white women's movement.' I would look just a little ridiculous sitting in their living rooms saying 'we this, we that.'"

Maracle feels that white feminists discriminate the first Nations women. The whites do not even accept the first Nations females as women. They invite the first Nations women with the intention of sensitizing if the topic is racism. They expect the first Nations woman 'to retain our position well below them as their servants. We are not as a matter of course, invited as an integral part of 'their movement—the women's movement'" (*I Am Woman* 20-21). Donna Landry and Gerald MacLean opine, "Because (white feminists) are not acquainted with traditions outside their own cultures and histories, the ideological and the theatrical legacies that they write from inevitably deny as valid any modes of struggle and organization which have their origins in non-European philosophical traditions." (183)

This view is upheld by Canadian first Nations playwright Monique Mojica who conveys through *Princess Pocahontas and the Blue Spots* that feminism cannot be treated as a homogenous movement in conditions of colonialism and individual suppression. The international women's day cannot be accepted by a third world woman until 'feminist shoes' accommodate her 'wide square brown feet' allowing her to 'feel the earth through their soles' (58). Since gender functions along with race, class and culture, the discrimination in these spaces is co-lateral. As M.F. Salat says, 'between what Alice Walker has called 'womanism' and white dominated 'feminism' the difference is colour' (128)

Since the first Nations associations turned out to conceptualize on the gender-oriented perceptions of society and nationhood, perpetuating the subordination of women, their women could not draw any assistance from them in their struggle for gender equality and racial discrimination.

Though Mardi is central in the American Indian movement, her centrality is ignored by the movement. Armstrong props up Mardi to expose the general significance attributed to women activists in their struggle for decolonization (*Slash*). To Armstrong, these writings of historic actualities have a therapeutic effect.

The First Nations women's participation with the issues of the white community will be looked upon with suspicion by First Nations men, no matter how well intentioned the women's participation is. So they resist conflating tensions between the American Indian movement, which may dissipate the solidarity of their community. However disintegration from the white feminism does not mean homogeneity in the first Nations female fraternity .First Nations writer Nicole Brossard contends that because the oppressor and the oppressed, male and female, live in the same culture 'most of the time they [women] are already integrated or neutralized by institutions such as marriage and heterosexism' (Williamson 67). Though there is an increase in the number of educated and competent women, most of them are lax to step into spaces that are outside the circle of their profession.

Sexual stereotyping should be discouraged in the upbringing of children. Societal disintegration is affected in the reserve areas where women's condition is deteriorating due to the failing economy, illiteracy and unemployment.

Women have to emerge from their state of dependence through their organizations to overcome the problems resulting from the dichotomies of issues. The traditional role attributed to women is child-bearing, child-rearing and serving the family. The ecofeminists' definition of women as basically biological beings tend to uphold the androcentric scientific 'discoveries' in support of the secondary role attributed to women. Instead of designing curricula to solely meet the needs of the industrial economy, community interests should be coordinated to ensure the retention of the culture, language and tradition of the First Nations.

Ethnic writers of the colonial world like Beatrice Culleton, Jeannette Armstrong, Maria Campbell, Lee Maracle, Beth Brant and Alice Walker took up the task of challenging female subjugation. They are involved in a counter identification process by challenging the politics of gender and attempting to reinstate women in their former positions of power. The female protagonists of their texts resist the impositions on them and attempt to establish their identity in Canadian society. Varying narratological techniques are employed by these writers to combat the Racism and sexism of their society.

Pamela Boyd through her play *Inside Out* (1987) draws public attention to the traumatic situation of women in familial bond. Ellen, the thirty-five-year-old female protagonist is denied her identity by her chauvinistic husband. Her motherly love for her baby foils her attempts to establish her identity. The writer highlights the frustrations of women in contemporary society.

As the counter-movement against colonization gathered momentum, more female writers realized the need to voice the double marginalization experienced by First Nations women in the colonial context. Their struggles began achieving their goals by the 1960s. The first landmark in these struggles was attained in 1985 when the equality of men and women was guaranteed under Section 35 of the Charter of Rights. Bill C-31 came into effect in 1985 that was meant to restore Indian status to Indian women who had married non-Indians. This Bill further guarantees the band's authority to determine membership.

Feminist writer Sheelagh Convey points out that the Canadian literature institutions are discriminatory to women writers. Keeshing Tobias expressed the view that literary institutions determine the value of literary works based on Canada's male dominant middle class white culture. Anything else is an ancillary or at worst an aberration (*Globe and Mail* 26 May).

Social problems like deplorable living conditions and health programs in the reserves were the primary issues raised by feminist activists of the First Nations, even though they had not reached any coordination in their struggles. Soon they realized that the female voice is not sufficiently heard, the patriarchy turns a deaf ear to them. This deafness was visible from the authorities when women spoke. However the First Nations upheld their traditional trust in the capabilities of women, when they were represented by a woman—Ellen Gabriel for negotiations with the Canadian government in the Oka Conflict in 1990.

For the advancement of women's conditions, the psychological and social perceptions of the society ought to be altered. The First Nations feminist writers employ in their writings strategies like parody and subversion to dismantle notions of authority. One is the reintroduction of the Trickster. Maracle stresses the need for the recapture of the Trickster in First Nations women's writings. In Joan Crate's 'Pale as Real Ladies' (1990) this concept is discernible (184). The act of life writing by First Nations writers problematizes the patriarchal equations. Daphne Narlatt opines: 'to write a whole autobiography, I mean in its largest sense of self writing life . . . the whole truth, is to reach for what is almost unwritable, a hole in that other sense' (*Autobiography*). Writers who realized the need for a feminine voice maintain that the silence of women is taken for their objectification. They have to reclaim their lost voice and for that they have to express whatever opinions they have, whether they are accepted or not. The silence of women allows phallocracy to define women on the basis of their patriarchal affiliations. The observation of Emma LaRocque is pertinent in this context. In *Writing the Circle* (1990), she states that First Nations women were 'Wordless' and when they talk their words are politically and literally negated. Their concerns and needs were determined and articulated by their husbands and fathers, missionaries and government agents' (Preface xv). When the ethnic writers attempt to develop a counter discourse by projecting the First Nations culture and tradition, feminist writers like Maracle and Slipperjack attempt to dismantle the hierarchies of race, class and gender transforming the theoretical presuppositions and the imperialist assumptions of the whites. In attempting the erasure of power differentials, conditions for hegemonic dominance, Lee Maracle is very prominent among the First Nations. Though she began writing with ethnic issues, the experience of the double marginalization brought forth the urge to fight for gender equality. In *I Am Woman*, Maracle attempts a redefinition of women and to demarcate a space for women within the circle. Maracle states in the preface to the Second Edition of *I Am Woman*:

> *I Am Woman* represents my personal struggle with womanhood, traditional spiritual beliefs and political sovereignty written during a time when this struggle was not over. I had settled on very little when I first wrote *I Am Woman* except this: I and other native [sic] women ought to come by our perceptions of spirituality, culture, womanhood and sovereignty, from a place free of sexist and racist influence. (vii)

Maracle's writings are a struggle for women's self-actualization in the patriarchal oriented society. Her experience of gender bias makes her fight for the cause of women and she asserts herself through her writings. The dynamics of feminism is explored throughout *I Am Woman.*

Consequent to the organized pressure by women, some legislative changes are effected. The Supreme Court's ruling in 1988 of the Abortion Law being unconstitutional is an example. Equal Value Legislation Bill was passed by the Manitoba government in 1985. Salina Shrofel observes that discriminatory provisions continue to animate the law in its legislation, execution and jurisdiction (108-18). Although women comprised only four percent of people involved in sex for money, they form sometimes around seventy five percent of those arrested and charged for the crime. Even in these statistics the over-representation of First Nations women is a pointer at the negative impacts of phallocracy and colonization. Feminists argue that for eliminating the crime of the commodification of sexuality, the customers should be punished and the poor women should be relieved of the burden of discriminatory law (Boyle and Noonan).

As the First Nations feminist's movement gathered momentum, they faced the opposition from their own men. Many phallocentric organizations of the First Nations community fear that the successes of women's equality arguments may ultimately result in the undermining of the special protections guaranteed by the Indian Acts. They argued that by activating women's issues, much of the solidarity of the First Nations communities is lost in voicing the First Nations cause. Their position was that women also should join hands in the struggle for the entire First Nations. But women felt that they were treated as non-entities by their men. Glenna Perley remarks about the treatment meted out by feminist activists when they voiced their problem before the chief. 'The chief treated us like we were invisible' (qtd. Silman 124). Feminist confrontations of male chauvinism is explicit in Armstrong's *Slash.* The male narrator tells how they, as First Nations male students, had ignored the girls. "None of the girls ever got asked to dance at the sock hops because us guys wouldn't" (35). In Culleton's *April Raintree*, it was Cheryl's husband who forces her into prostitution, which leads into her suicide as the typical example of the 'Native girl syndrome' of which the girl had been accused of by Mrs. Semple, the White social worker in their childhood. Maracle resents the fact that even First Nation men have come to believe that their women are beasts of burden (*I Am Woman* 17). She in turn attributes this beastliness to men. She asks: "How many times do you hear from our own brothers; Indian women don't whine and cry around, nag or complain. At least not the 'real' or 'true' Indian women. Embodied in that kind of language is negation of our femininity—the denial of our womanhood is the reduction of the whole people to a subhuman level." (20)

Maracle asserts: 'There is no single racism but a multiplicity of racism' (69). The title character in *Bobbi Lee* is devoid of any organizational affiliations. Still she confronts racism in many parts of the Americas. In her childhood she endures racism from the Whites and in consequence she hates all Whites. When she happens to be in a Mexican town their also she encounters 'Blatant racism' (53) from the Mexicans. She says that the Mexican felt superior to the Indians and ill-treated the Indians. This forces her to the conclusion that racism is common place 'an accepted way of life' (54).

First Nations feminist writers' zeal to find a space for them in the centre sphere received added vigor in Maracle:

> I am a burning flame
> Not yet unhurt
> Not yet Women
> But very much alive. (*I Am Woman* 16).

Maracle feels that the racial predilection of whites have driven Native Women's subjugation to 'Subhuman levels' (20), which has coloured even the white women's attitude towards them. She blames women themselves for this predicament. They attribute greater prowess to men. 'We look at males when they speak and stare off into space when a woman steps assertively into the breach of leadership' (18).

April experiences the denial of her identity at her white husband's household both by patriarchy and White hegemony. After the rape, her assailant justifies his action by negating her womanhood that she did not protest his advances. April is victim of the Europeans' racism and sexism that ultimately charges power into her to accept her identity and to assert the right of herself as well as her people. At April's white husband's house, a white woman openly asks April's Sister Cheryl, about her hyphenated identity. Cheryl refuses the denial of Canadian identity and the imposed label of Métis:

> 'What is the proper word for people like you?'
> Cheryl replies 'Woman.'
> The White woman asks again.
> 'No, No, I mean Nationality.'
> Cheryl again evades the label Métis
> And says. 'Oh, I'm sorry. We are Canadians.' (91)

Cheryl would have proudly accepted her Métis identity if the white lady had not been imposing her hegemonic stand on her. The Whites, even though they were only a settler community, deny the First Nations people their identity as Canadian and prefer to refer to them with their more denigrating hyphenated identities.

> Maracle's struggles begin with the therapy of confession. She points out: I used to be uncomfortable being with women. I can remember saying to a close friend of mine that I had more men friends than women. She nodded. Yes, unoffended, but none of us could think of a single male to whom we could say the reserve without offending his manhood. We both had become complicit in the erasure of ourselves as women, as Native. (*I Am Woman* 19)

Maracle's perception is that Native Women had been denigrated to 'subhuman' status and 'have been the object of a kind of sexual release of white males whose appetites are too gross for their own Women' (*Ibid.* 18) and she expresses the enormity of the First Nations women's predicament: 'We have but one right, the right to die at our own hands whenever we choose to pull the plug' (*Ibid.* 71).

In unison with the First Nations feminist voices of Canada Toni Morrison, the Black American writer, depicts the sufferings of Black women in America under the subjugatory tactics of the whites, exposing the universality of the racism of white colonizers.

Parody is employed by Joan Crate as a tactic to resist the racial and sexist stereotyping of First Nations in White discourse and their ideology of femininity in her poem *Pale as Real Ladies: Poems of Pauline Johnson* (1989). In Jovette Marchessault's *Mother of Grass* (1989) we find a decentring of the patriarchal assumptions conceptualized in Western myths and through the construction of the character grandmother, matrilineage is attempted challenging the western ideology, to attain the lost world of female divinity.

Beth Brand's *A Long Story* (1988) is a powerful indictment of the double standards of society on race and gender. When a First Nations man has to struggle against the imperial impositions, a First Nations woman has to fight the impositions of imperialism along with the impositions of patriarchy and the white feminist impositions. Some writers even write against the racially hegemonic white feminist writers who maintain racial exclusiveness. Bell Hooks mimics the White feminist's stand: 'Do not speak in the voice of resistance only speak for that space in the margin that is a sigh of deprivation, a wound, an unfulfilled longing. Only speak your pain.' (23)

First Nations women writers face the antagonism of the mainstream writers. Some even express their discontent at the First Nations writers' occupying more and more space in the Canadian literary Diaspora. Frank Davey states: 'With what appears to be at least the temporary suspension of a national culture and a national literary audience, it has been extremely difficult for any Canadian poet not discursively affiliated with some regional, feminist, ethnic, racial or otherwise ideological community to find audience recognition or identity.' (6)

Alongside their fights for gender equality and cultural identity, Indian women still play their traditional role under the changed circumstances as nurturers and supporters of the family, educators and transmitters of culture (Dion 114).

> Benita parry challenges Spivak statement 'the subaltern cannot speak': Since the Native woman is constructed within multiple social relationships and positioned as the product of different class, caste and cultural specifications, it should be possible to locate traces and testimony of women's voices on those sites where women inscribed themselves as healers, ascetics singers of sacred songs, artisans and artists and by this to modify Spivak's model of the silent subaltern.(185).

Through the character Alice in *Like a Child of the Earth*, Jovette Marchessault points a finger at the traditional notions of silence and propriety imposed on woman: "Alice never had doubts about anything, because doubt was disastrous for women. Women were made to believe in and obey the sublime. It was much better to be taken for naïve, even crazy then to disobey. Alice wouldn't even talk about it. To her faith was an action and doubt a thought." (163) Alice was a representative of the typical hardworking First Nations woman of Canada who laboured in the homesteads of Europeans for a living. The narrator says that from her parents she 'learned to keep her mouth shut' (133).

In *Laundry Basket* (1993), Maracle treats the topic of racism and humiliation experienced by a First Nations woman at the hands of her white husband; however she resists the racist oppression with the power of the true First Nations woman. In her poem 'Indian Woman' (*Breath Tracks* 106-7) Armstrong urges First Nations women to establish their identity through cultural affirmation and escape the rejection and self-hatred they lived through years of colonization.

In her interview with Janice Williamson, Armstrong claims that she has juxtaposed the dual images of the First Nations woman—the pejorative 'squaw,' how other people see them and the real First Nations woman, so that they can see and understand themselves and pass on that to their posterity. Armstrong believes that 'because the women are the central backbone of the family and the next generation' healing should be effected in them 'before healing in the family and outward to the rest of the community' (Williamson 9-10). They should not be victims of internalized racism.

After centuries of denigration and subjugation Indian women have become powerful enough to fight for the change of their predicament. They no longer rely on the government of patriarchal systems to determine their fate. They have acquired a collective voice and are relentlessly fighting for their rights. Maracle's words 'the voices of the unheard cannot help but be of value' *(I Am Woman* 1) is pertinent in the contemporary situation. First Nations women writers' today attempt to occupy the centre of Canadian discourse and empower their women. The great service rendered by feminist organizations is making women visible. Daphne Marlott observes, 'We live in two worlds, the one defined for us and that defined by us' (Godard, *Gynocritics* 3). Now Indian women are contributing unstinting services in solving society issues such as unemployment, alcohol abuse, abuse of women and children, family violence and health problems.

The attitude of women about themselves also has to change. Imparting higher education to women should be given primacy. Through education women can be equipped to be self-dependent. As Barbara Godard puts it: 'Change in the perspective influx a disjunction in the relation of perception between the seer and the scene, the subjective 'eye'/ I and the represented world, as they are related to each other, but also as they relate to the source of perceiving consciousness outside.' (*Politics* 200)

Writ(Right)ing as Resistance

> If this is history, how come so many Indian tribes were wiped out? How come they haven't got their land anymore? How come their food supplies were wiped out?. . . your history books don't say how the White people destroyed the Indian way of life. That's all [sic] you white people can do is teach a bunch of lies to cover your own tracks. (Beatrice Culleton, *April Raintree* 57)

From the 1950s onwards, psychological studies were made, especially by intellectuals from Third world countries, on the structures of imperialism and its impact on colonized peoples. These structures are generally accepted as postcolonial theories. The term postcolonial can be employed to describe cultural productions of the colonial world that reflect the political affectivity of their period that was 'both a consequence of and reaction to European imperial process' (Pandurang 5), which Barbara Harlowe brands as 'resistance literature' (28).

Though Stephen Slemon uses postcolonialism solely on the cultural context (14), Alan Lawson defines it differently: Postcolonialism 'is a politically motivated historical-analytical movement [which] engages with, resists and seeks to dismantle the effects of colonialism in the material, historical, cultural, political, pedagogical, discursive and textual domains.' (156).

Theorists on postcolonialism agree with the idea that postcolonial writings register resistance to the imperial agenda of control of the colonies. If colonialist discourse 'functions as a marker of subordination,' postcolonial discourse is a 'marker of identity, voice and hence empowerment' (Tiffin and Lawson 230). In order to deconstruct the manipulations in their representations, First Nations writers resorted to expressing their perspective, mostly in the form of life writing, which is also named fictional autobiography, fiction theorique (Brossard) autobiography (Gagman) and fictionalysis (Marlatt).

The writings of women writers stand out as a distinctive class as they are a doubly marginalized group. Barbara Harlowe observes that the texts by First Nations women writers resist the conventional literary genres and classifications like minority, Native etc. Their literary output is classed as 'writings' rather than fiction or nonfiction. Their semi-fictional writings represent their political affectivity of the period and by writing about it they express resistance to colonial subjugation (Resistance 28).

Prominent among the women writers in Canada who ventured on life writing 'breaking generations of silence . . . by naming the oppressors, the process of oppression' (Currie 150-51) leading to a therapeutic effect are Maria Campbell, Beatrice Culleton, Jeannette Armstrong, Lee Maracle, Jovette Marchessault, Ruby Slipper Jack etc., to name a few. The First Nations writers pursue the deconstructive process of taking the subject position by upsetting the binary oppositions in the colonial hierarchy, offering a diversity of articulation.

Although articulation of the experience of colonization is the core of all colonial writings, diversities in colonial conditions persist because of regional variations. To Armstrong, life writing is part of the First Nations struggle to 'uncurl from the somnambulistic fetal ball, survival state that psychological oppression had reduced our peoples to, in the aftermath of the totalitarianistic measures to dispossess our peoples of everything that is meaningful in life' (Foreword *Bobbi Lee* 15).

The resistance writings help to assert the self-definitions of the First Nations in the colonized world. By remaining a binding force among the peoples, they attempt to recuperate the lost history, culture, language and religious identity of the First Nations, exhorting them to fight against colonialism and regain their lost status. Lee Maracle observes: 'Once we understand what kind of world they have created then we can figure out what kind of world we can recreate' (*I Am Woman* 116). La Rocque justifies that the First Nations are compelled to 'Self express because there was so much about our history and about our lives that . . .has been disregarded, infantilized and falsified' (Lutz 181).

Applaudable attempts have been made by the First Nations women writers in establishing a space for the women of their community, telling their own stories; they are attempting to dispel the impositions and constructions on them. Because they are unwritten, First Nations History lost the truth-value in the European sense and Europeans classify First Nations history as myths and legends and disclaim them. Stimulated by imperial acculturation, postcolonial writers develop a plurality of histories and culture and promulgate their versions of history and the cultural context of events through their writings to refuse and refute the histories promulgated by the imperialists. Lee Maracle observes that though the First Nations did not have a common history, language and customs, they have 'a commonality and a common dream' (Williamson 176). She claims to 'rewrite her life into the pages of a new history' through her text, *I Am Woman* (121).

Though imperial history suggests that there wasn't any resistance to imperial ingress, counter discursive history dismisses this suggestion, projecting the demoralizing colonial experience of the First Nations and exposes the rhetoric of the colonizers as manipulation.

With a view to exposing the injustice inflicted on her society by the European settlers, Maria Campbell traces the history of some of the First Nations families in the Prince Albert region of Saskatchewan. She presents an exegesis of how those families became destitute and forced to live on the side of roads living as 'Squatters on road allowance land' (*Halfbreed* 8).

Culleton confronts the lies in imperial history propagated by the whites. They teach these lies to students in classrooms. She illustrates how it affected the First Nations. Once Cheryl, April's sisters had a confrontation with her teacher, when they were taught 'how the Indians scalped, tortured and massacred brave white explorers and missionaries,' Cheryl loudly asserted that 'it was all a bunch of lies.' She asks:

> If this is history, how come so many Indian tribes were wiped out? How come they haven't got their land anymore? How come their food supplies were wiped out? . . .Your History books don't say how the white people destroyed the Indian way of life. That's all (sic) you white people can do is teach a bunch of lies to cover your own tracks. (57)

Cheryl's confrontation with the manipulated history brought her severe punishment. When still she stuck on to her stand, her white foster mother was called in, to subdue her. And she used the threat of separating her from her sister, to control her.

Maracle writes about a similar confrontation. She challenges the portrayal of Louis Riel as 'a mad man that was hanged' and asserts that she could not 'forsake' her 'ancestors'(*Sojourner's Truth* 111). Campbell rejects the accepted versions of the Riel Rebellion (1885) and the Red River Rebellion (1869), by pointing out the manpower, machinery and money expended by the colonial government to suppress and silence some hundred and fifty Métis warriors under Louis Riel (*Halfbreed* 6). To bring to light the First Nations version of their history, Culleton employs tactics like Cheryl's letters to her sister April. First Nations grandmothers like Cheechum in Campbell's *Halfbreed* contribute to their recording of oral history and struggle for self-determination.

Jovette Marchessault maintains that European savagery on the First Nations ensued since the time of Columbus. 'Language' and 'voice' had been 'weapons' of First Nations when Columbus and his crew came to the Americas (*Like a child of the earth* 34). He enjoyed the hospitality of the people and left. When Columbus visited the First Nations for a second time, he attempted to intimidate the people by unleashing a large Spanish dog on them: 'Many Indians perished. Those who resisted were attacked and taken alive and were sent to Spain as slaves. Many of them died on the way. The others were sold in the market as slaves.' (*Ibid.* 41-42).

The Indians preferred to flee to the mountains where they poisoned themselves with manioc sap rather than work as Columbus's slaves. The regimes were rapidly depopulated. 'The conquerors had left with their cross and their greed. They returned with gold, slaves and syphilis.' With bitter sarcasm Marchessault refers to the 'pioneer's slaughter of the bison that had been sustaining the people and the landscape' (*Ibid.* 42). In Beatrice Culleton's *Spirit of the White Bison* (1984), this irrational slaughter of the bison is thematized. Along with the bison, other animals and birds also disappeared (*Ibid.* 136).

American First Nations writer Janet Campbell Hale throws light on the history incidents at Wounded Knee through the recollections of the title character in *The Jailing of Cecelia Capture* (1985). "There were photographs of the massacre. It happened long after the battles, long after the treaties were signed. . . . They were much worse than anything she had seen from My Lai. The Indian bodies lay frozen in the snow and they were not the bodies of warriors. They were all kinds of people, old people, women, and children. None of them was armed. They were gunned down by the U.S. Army at Wounded Knee." (167)

In *Sundogs* (1992) Maracle points out the various repressive measures effected on the First Nations community: 'Organized violence, conquest by sword and mascot, organized child stealing through the school system and the child welfare Act, apprehension, terror, defamation of national character, racism, alcohol poisoning, imprisonment, hanging, language [sic] and cultural prohibition total racial invalidation.' (69)

The First Nations fight back with their only weapon 'dogged

insistence on truth.' Maracle's protagonist Marianne's family earnestly supports Elijah Harper's obstruction of the Meech Lake Accord (69).

The confrontations of First Nations reality and struggles for existence and the fights of the First Nations to survive as a people leads Penny, Armstrong's protagonist in *Whispering in Shadows* (2000).

Natasha Kzanzek observes that there is irony in the fact that the destroyers preserve specimens of 'vanishing ways of life' in their museums and commercialese it. The missionaries and enforcers who penetrate into another space and plunder another people are given heroic dimensions and are eulogized as 'defenders of the Empire.' The observations on the exhibits at the Royal Ontario Museum speak volumes on the barbarity of the Europeans in their habit of souvenir collection. Though it sounds so innocuous, these souvenirs stand as a symbol of the violation done on the peoples of the Empire by the Europeans. They are representative of the history of destruction by the explorers and missionaries on these lands (Itwaru and Kzanzek 80).

Natasha Kzanzek offers resistance to the imperialist construction of images by effecting a re-reading of Conrad's *Heart of Darkness*. Though the narrator of *Heart of Darkness* expresses awareness of the European imperialist designs, he himself is not free of the imperialist's racist assumptions and uses a number of clichés prevalent in the 'Empire Imaginary' (83).

Though lasciviousness is imposed as part of the image of the First Nations, Natasha asserts that it is an attribute of the European settlers and Explorers. She contends for this alternative vision by pointing out that the Europeans fantasized that in the orient, there is no social constraint on their strange sexual excesses. This stimulus is reflected in the writings of the early traders and explorers. In the name of Christianizing and civilizing the African First Nations, the Missionaries had been exploiting them. Reverent A.W. Banfield's photograph of a young African woman and his exegesis of it tell implicitly his exploitation of the woman. She is the symbol of the nameless hunted animal and he is the hunter with the camera attempting to fix her into static space. Natasha points out that as in the imperial perception, this Reverent Banfield believed that he had a right to take the woman's 'image' and recontextualize it, disparaging her as 'primitive' (Itwaru and Kzanzek 85).As said observes, the 'overpowering' and 'domestication' of the orient\ female by masculine colonizer is unabashedly exhibited here (*Orientalism* 207).

The colonial government's shrewd policies to grant the land from First Nations peoples is thematized in many First Nations texts. Marianne in Maracle's *Sundogs* remembers how land dribbled through their hands by disease and hunger along with the application of laws by the Royal Commission. 'There are so few Indians left in this village that this commission recommends appropriation of the land and the transfer of the remaining stragglers to another reserve. It took only seventy-five years of settlement to destroy one thousand eight hundred villages by this process.' (156)

Armstrong's *Slash* (1985) is a historicizing of the political involvement of the First Nations through their organization, American Indian Movement (AIM) during the 1960 and 70s. The central character Slash challenges the European interpretations of First Nations cultures saying that 'we have our own interpretation as to how we function best' (223-24).

Maracle finds occasion to refer to the historic incident of the Mohawks standoff at Oka, blocking the bridge at Kanestake against building a golf course on the burial grounds of the Mohawks. She says 'I can't believe anyone would want to play golf on someone else's graveyards.' Further she adds: 'The press fills its pages with broadcasts full of ridiculous comments about how this is not going to do our land claims any good etc. Not a word about the shame the Quebec government and the town of Oka should feel about golfing on other peoples [sic] graves.' (*Sun-*

dogs 125-26)

In Bobbi, Lee Maracle again justifies the Mohawk's stand in the Oka crisis? 'At no time in history have Europeans ever suggested playing golf on their own graves. Yet grave site after gravesite of our dead are considered accessible for the most ridiculous of past times.' (8)

The Plains Indian Ledger Art implicitly points out the European atrocities on First Nations. Karen Daniels Peterson brings to light the causation of the origination of the Plains Indian Ledger Art. In 1874, seeing the settlers motiveless hunting down of the bison, certain Indian tribes broke out of their Reserves to protect the bison from extermination. The army hunted the men down and took arbitrary measures to suppress them. The government arrested seventy-two such men and branded them 'the most hostile' and put them in double chains. They were sent to Fort sill by chaining them to Wagons. En route to Fort Marion, 'One of the prisoners jumped out of the window of the train.' It could not be an attempt to escape, as his hands and legs were in chains. But the man was shot and killed. In April 1875 'Without a trial or a hearing' the prisoners were taken away 'to what they believed would be their execution.' These prisoners held at Fort Marion were provided with drawing materials by the officer in charge of them. They produced autobiographical sketches depicting their past tribal wars, their life in the plains. Some sketches represent even their life in the prison. These graphics later came to be referred to as Plains Indian Ledger Art (15). Thomas King in *Green Grass Running Water* (1993) refers to this event (20-21).

The European ethnocentric bias ignored the First Nations' modes of recording history through their oral, hieroglyphic, pictographic inscriptions on barks of trees, clothes, skins etc. Claude Levi Strauss maintains that sciences like anthropology come to the rescue of aboriginal history 'to reconstruct the history of peoples who have never known writing' (24).

As Linda Warley points out, 'the attempt to understand and articulate in writing one's own subjectivity involves an ongoing process of self-analysis and self-fashioning' (66). Deploying the technique of autobiography, Maracle attempts the act of decolonizing the self and thereby decolonizing the nation in *Bobbi Lee*. It charts the meaningless existence of Indian society and disintegration in the Sixties and Seventies through the life of a woman who faces the racism of the society in all spheres of life. Bobbi Lee encounters blatant racism during her stay at visa life in California. While working with different races during the grape harvest season, she felt racist intolerance from these people, who do not even pretend politeness (53). She realizes that 'there is no single racism but a multiplicity of racisms' (69). Marianne's experience was not different. She remembers the humiliation experienced by her by the whites undignified treatment of First Nations girls. Squaws are not dignified as the white girls. Anybody could take them for a ride was the general concept: 'Erase yourself or consent to shame. That is the sociology of the Native and woman in Canada. It is the result of besiegement, encroachment, small neglect, impoverishment and mass death. I had my mind and spirit crippled by the choices they left open to me as though there were no others.' (*Sundog* 161)

Both Campbell and Culleton challenge the accepted belief that in Canadian society racism is tolerable. Campbell points out the horrible treatment meted out by the First Nations in Canada during the onslaught of colonialism (Lutz 58-59). In *Halfbreed*, Campbell articulates the way in which racism and poverty are linked: how effective it is in subjugating and dominating colonized people. She talks indignantly about the racism, which forced her father even to become a poacher in the National park (59). The disempowerment leading to self-destruction is reflected in *I Am Woman* where Maracle underlines Jay Macpherson's argument that 'the personal is political.' 'Canadians are fed lies that blind them to their own truth and the light of human worthiness is doused by notions of superiority that inflames their distorted character. This process creates an artificial and tenuous loyalty to hierarchy, which is essentially murderous. (*Sundogs* 195)

Campbell remembers their visits to town in her childhood to sell their artifacts.' The whites 'insulted them and treated them as thieves' (*Halfbreed* 132). The Métis walked in the town with bent heads because of internalized racism, accepting the space of the 'other.' They could hear whites making 'mean and dirty' comments about Indians everywhere. LaRocque confesses: 'I became aware that I was part of a group that was 'open season' for anyone's misjudgments' and slurs' (*Tides* 114-15). Campbell mentions that though her family had been very hospitable and her mother had been a very pious Christian during the forty years they lived there, no white neighbour ever entered their house. Only three old Swedes visited them when their mother died (*Halfbreed* 13).

Juxtaposing the white world and the First Nations world in a small town, Maracle exposes in *Ravensong* (1993) the racism of the colonialists and the sufferings of the First Nations. The bridge ironically remains a symbol of distance and difference. Stacey is indignant of the indifference of the white people at sufferings of the First Nations. She could not evade the comparative concepts of the situation affected by the ravages of the flu epidemic. In the First Nations villages, 'men barely dressed in cedar bark wraps flew through the business of burying body after body.' The survivors failed to give their near and dear ones a proper burial, when in the white cities the attire of the people who attended the burial ceremony was so striking. They wore '[d]recent black' with matching 'patent leather shoes.' Hypocrisy marked even their grieving (14-15).

When the health department ignored the problem of the epidemic in the First Nations village, they made their own possible arrangements to face the situation. Even though modern medicine available at the time could easily check the spread of the disease, the government did nothing to save the First Nations population, which infuriated them. LaRocque blames the callousness of the authorities who remained blind to the First Nations who were dying of T.B. Though their hamlet was on the outskirts of the city, the immunization programme began only in the late 1950s (*Tides* 112).

As she was cruelly dehumanized and institutionalized in marriage, Campbell renounces her marriage (*Halfbreed* 133). April's experience was not different. She heard her white mother-in-law saying 'you never know how they're going to turn out. And I would simply dread being grandmother to a bunch of snivelling little half-breeds' (*April Raintree* 100). Bob's only reason for marrying her was just to get back at his mother. The denial of identity to the First Nations women fuels April's decision to establish her identity, after her failed marriage.

Though schooling had been forced on the First Nations children, schools remained centres of racist discrimination. LaRocque points out that before experiencing racism in the wider sphere of Canada, she had experienced racism at school. The textbooks were propagating the denigratory images (*Tides* 114). Armstrong's *Slash* met with this differential treatment. On the First day at school, the Indian students were kept back and the principal talking about the rules said: 'You Indians are lucky to be here. We'll get along just fine as long as you don't steal from the other kids. I want you all to wait here while the nurse comes to check your heads and ask you some questions.' (23-24)

The teachers except a few were prejudiced against Indian students (39). Armstrong recalls that the white kids teased the First Nations students at school Once a big fat white boy named Humphrey said 'you frigging Injuns are nothing but thieves, full of lice, everybody knows that! 'A First Nations boy named Monty provoked by the remark kicked Humphrey. Monty was dismissed from school with immediate effect but the white boy who started everything did not get any punishment (*Slash* 24).

Though Bobbi Lee had desired the friendship of the whites at school, their 'contempt and ostracism forced [her] to conclude that all whites were the same: creepy, cruel, racist' (37). When a classmate, an English girl took Bobbi Lee to her house, the girl's mother scolded the girl for taking an Indian to their house, 'What do you think you're doing bringing this Indian into the Lynn residence? Don't you know we don't want Indians here! The poor girl started crying.' (49)

The white were inhuman and callous to make dehumanizing stereotypes of Indians. LaRocque expresses concern at the future of Indians who are brought up internalizing the negative stereotypes imposed on them. 'What may happen to Native persons who grow up with comics, textbooks and movies that objectify Indian as wild and violent?' Women become the most targeted victims of this kind of violence and dehumanization (*Tides* 121). By the hybridization of the genres of autobiography and fiction, Armstrong's *Slash* is a reaccentuation of the historic events of the struggles of the American Indian movement for the rights of Indians. Colonialisms internalized oppression is central to *Slash*, where racial and sexual oppressions intersect.

There are divergent interests among the colonized. When some uphold the First Nations' culture and traditions, some 'want to try all kinds of new stuff and be more like white people.' Some feel caught between two worlds. Tommy tells his friend Jimmy, 'I don't know who is right anymore.' His life in the city makes him more confused. The much-orchestrated 'development' only contributes to the advantage of the white community at the expense of the First Nation's community (42-43).

Slash and his friends Jimmy are dichotomized. When Slash wants to regain the pride of the First Nations, Jimmy idealizes the white man and wants to assimilate. Jimmy defines the Indians in terms of the white perceptions and is ashamed of the inadequacies of the Indians. He tries to dissociate himself from the

Indian society and justifies his negation of his people and culture: 'I like to feel good. I feel good when white friends of mine talk and joke with me as if I were like them. They only do that if I wear smart pants and shoes and have money to play pool with. I don't like them to think I'm like the rest of the Indians. I wish our people were like them. . . . I hate being an Indian. I hate Indian ways' (44).

The sense of alienation generated by the imposition of colonization was traumatizing to the First Nations. Many try to escape the inadequacies by attempting assimilation. April takes the resolution:

> When I grow up I wouldn't be poor. I'd be rich. Being a half-breed meant being poor and dirty. It meant being weak and having to drink. It meant being ugly and stupid. It meant living off white people. . . . When I go free from being a foster child, then [sin] I would live just like a real white person. (*April Raintree* 34)

April denies her Métis identity because she has become ashamed of that identity, having grown up in a society where the First Nation girls are accused of the 'Native girl Syndrome' (48). As the social worker Mrs. Semple had mentioned. In his attempt to assimilate with the white society, Jimmy tried to get a 'clean job' by studying accounting, and going with a white girl. All his attempts to shake off everything Indian, isolates him in the Indian society and he is unacceptable in the white society too. Although Jimmy qualifies himself for the 'good clean job' (*Slash* 83) as he had envisaged he experiences the negation and discrimination from the whites. To the whites, Jimmy does not differ from the rest of the 'drunken lazy Indians.' He realizes that being victims of the internalized oppression, the Indians are not good for cram jobs. They hire some 'ex DIA goat.' (221)

Like many others of her generation, Campbell admired the white society and desired assimilation, only to be disillusioned. She realizes that the First Nations who had similar dreams and admiration for the whites were all defeated by the colonizing powers (*Halfbreed* 27).

Unlike Jimmy, the awareness of colonial oppression arouses Slash and he attempts to fight the situation. Slash says that the First Nations attempt assimilation because of their image of inferiority (221). He openly challenges the promise of a 'great society' by President John F. Kennedy and sees further discrimination of the First Nations in the exhortation 'to reject any among us who seek to re-open old wounds and rekindle hatreds' (168). There is an underlying suggestion to suppress the First Nations who are offering resistance to the centuries-old discrimination they have been suffering. Instead of justice and equality for all, Slash sees in the words of the President further denial and denigration of the First Nations. He feels that only those who are willing to assimilate can exist in American society. If assimilation is not possible, they have to vanish. "Down memory lane, Debra Swallow has the pain and shame felt by the Métis community at the label Half-breed. In her childhood she had fought against white girls for calling her 'half-breed'" (Beth Brant, *Gathering of Spirit* 44)

Cheryl resists the exclusionary thrust in the label Métis when a white woman asked her 'what is the proper word for people like you' (*April Raintree* 116). The questioner implicitly denies her Canadian nationality. In Culleton, the two choices left to the Indians are represented by the two sisters. April attempts assimilation but gets disillusioned by the bitter experiences of racism and sexism; Cheryl who attempts the 'third choice' and upholds her Métis identity becomes a gutter creature and finally commits suicide.

Maracle's *I Am Woman* is an excoriation of the racism and sexism of the whites; in *Sundogs* she upholds the observations of Fanon on the racism of the whites;

> The portrait of the colonized as lazy, criminal and dumb was a

> construction of the colonizers' prejudices and anxieties. There was no truth to it; but instead a reflection of the need to rationalize racial and political subjugation. The colonizers' violence was not a hereditary trait but the result of the psychological and material violence of the colonial relation. (qtd. Gordon 105)

Armstrong resents, 'It's a total shame the way they always treat Indians as if we were dogs or something' (*Slash* 158). She points out that the Ottawa march by the First Nations had been peaceful. But infiltrators gave the tint of violence and when the organizers failed to check it, the riot police charged on the marchers. 'It seemed that they were waiting for a chance to move in as soon as they could. . . . It almost was like they had been told to use as much violence as they wanted on the Indians.' Although thousands of pictures on the police violence had been taken only 'tame versions' appeared in papers (156-157). Maracle stresses that video films show that the arrest of the road blockers at Kanestake was 'anything but peaceful' (*Sundogs* 270). The dualistic constructs of the law served to legitimize the subjugatory tactics of colonial domination and to keep the First Nations in a low profile.

The suppressive policies instill violence in Slash. He is a victim of the self-hatred resulting from inferiorization. His violent outbursts and constant movement are the outcome of this brimming self-hatred. Mardy is the one who succeeds in creating the right political awareness in Slash. When he was about to be sentenced for imprisonment, he happened to meet her, who is an activist of the Indian Friendship centre.

Their organization, the Red Patrol, is trying to provide a third choice by creating pride in the Indian in claiming their identity. Elders like pra-cwa believe that upholding Indian culture and spirituality is the solution to the problems faced by Indians due to European colonization.

When the contextual and comparative concepts of racism call for the assimilationist tactics, Slash points out that if his people are happy with their way of life, why should it be changed like that of the whites? He realizes that he can succeed by reviving the past. The traditional practices, medicine etc. of the Indians should be revived. The medical ways of his people gave him a renewed self: 'All the questions that were unanswered for years suddenly seemed too simple . . . it wasn't a matter of belief. It was more it knowing for sure' (201). The treatment he underwent under the traditional ways makes him a changed person and he feels strong and empowered. He finds himself powerful enough to heal his father. The empowerment is affected by the recognition and revival of the past.'

'Colonial power was buttressed by the production of knowledge about colonized cultures which endlessly produced a degenerate image of the Orient for those in the west, or occident' (Macleod 22). Hence cultural specificity and the elements that symbolize the cultural heritage are being reclaimed by the colonized to establish their identity and to make themselves visible in the postcolonial societies.

Absence of the pronouns like he/ she in the First Nations language, amply subscribe to the finding that First Nations societies were egalitarian. Patriarchal culture of the whites has its negative impact on the First Nations culture. The white men used to abuse their wives. In the earlier First Nations societies, if a man abused his wife, he would be warned by the relatives of the woman. But in colonial societies, men took it as a privilege to abuse their wives. Women became unable to resist the male abuse, a trait Maracle finds as the negative effect of the Residential school system (*Ravensong* 149-50).

Paula Gunn Allen connects colonialism and sexism and sees its effects on Native societies: "The physical and cultural genocide of American Indian tribes was and is mostly about patriarchal fear of gynocracy. . . . The colonizers saw that as long as women held unquestioned power of such magnitude, attempts at total conquest of the continent were bound to fail" (*Sacred Hoop*

3).

The diversities of the First Nations and colonial cultural codes had its stringencies on First Nations life and many found standing between two worlds. Stacey finds it hard to balance the morals of the white society and that of her own society. Her mother's revelation that her children are her husband's brother's children becomes unacceptable to Stacey. Being brought up in the white world Stacey judges the morals of her mother with the whites' yardstick. However she recognizes that in her mother's own 'world of choice and acceptance, (she) was safe' (*Ravensong* 106). Maracle stresses the Native custom: 'It was unseemly for single men to visit single women in their homes, unattended by a male relative unless he was moving in for good; yet should a young girl have a child without a man no sanctions existed to make her account for her indiscretion.' (87) Pursuance of the white way of life compelled First Nations to abandon their traditional way of life, which gradually resulted in their dispossession and marginalization.

Marianne's mother is uncompromising to the white community. She persists in the presumption that because of the white invaders, the cultural genocide of the First Nations is effected. She constantly raves at the white men for the First Nations disempowerment. 'You have done everything to us; robed us, raped us, pillaged us, until we are no more. No morals, No culture, just a bunch of raggedy Indians' (*Sundogs* 135). But some like Bertha in Maracle's *Sojourners Truth* get lost, as they are unable to fight back.

Taking a shift from the 'other' to the 'I,' Joan Create attempts to construct a self from the fragments. She portrays the cultural schizophrenia experienced by the First Nations consequent of colonization, by projecting the image of the 'drunken Indian' in the white constructs (*Breathing Water*). The memories of Owl, the textual voice in Slipperjack's *Honor the Sun* (1987) portrays the simple pleasures and innocent joys of the First Nations community, before the colonial subjugation. The nostalgia for that lost world covertly suggests the denial and marginalization experienced by the First Nations. The Fort Marion Ledger Arts is an assertion of First Nations culture, which forms part of their arsenal against the onslaught of First Nations culture by the Europeans. The most sacred of the First Nations cultural configuration is the Sundance. It is a communal festival celebrated outdoors.

Maracle in *Sundogs* presents the Sweat Ceremony of the First Nations as part of the recuperation of the First Nations cultural practices. To renew his damaged self, Armstrong's character Slash participates in the Sweat Ceremony, and revives himself. Knowing the worth of the ceremony, he takes his father to it finding that his father is gradually becoming a 'gutter creature' after the death of his son Danny. Armstrong contends that the First Nations' culture and philosophy are relevant in the contemporary society, 'Where individualism is causing social chaos and where people are killing the environment out of individual selfish need' (Williamson 10).

Oren Lyons, a First Nations' Elder, points out that 'caring for each other is our highest calling . . .helping each other is the shortcut to spirituality.' Lyons maintains that spirituality is related to our relationships with the environment and society. Mutual respect and respect for mother Earth are the source of mental peace: 'In our way of life, in our government, with every decision we make, we always keep in mind the seventh generation to come. Its [sic] our job to see that the people coming ahead the generations still unborn, have a world no worse than ours and hopefully better.' (Wall and Arden 68) Oren Lyon stresses that disobeying the structures will result in the destruction of our own existence (*Ibid.* 66).

A councillor of one of the Bands in Armstrong's *Slash* warns the authorities about the danger of polluting water sources by the use of chemicals. It pollutes the environment and destroys the ecology (216). Our ancestors had developed methods to preserve the ecological balance. As Clarkson and others point out, 'all living creatures had to be cognizant of the structure of the day, the cycle of the seasons, and their effects on all other living matter' (4).

Marchessault mentions how the Europeans destroy the ecological balance by their material pursuits. She bewails the loss of the rich natural resources like the buffalo. Pre-colonial Canada had been a world of plenty, which had been destroyed by the Europeans who slaughtered the buffalo and other beings just for fun (*Child of the Earth* 110, 134). The anthropocentric Euro cultures do not attribute any value to lives other than humans on earth. Marchessault registers sorrow at the fate of the animals and birds sent to space in spacecraft, in the name of experimenbitation (*White Pebbles* 53). With the European settlement 'the bison disappeared. . . . The Wolf, Beaver, Fox, Bear and Frog clans were decimated' (*Child of the Earth* 137). Beatrice Culleton elaborates on the indiscrete slaughter of the buffalo, which resulted in the extinction of the species. In *Spirit of the White Bison* (1984), she effectively presents the perspective of the animals and the First Nation in this regard.

Again, in the medical field, First Nations began to receive reprisals. Their cures failed against the imported diseases. When the flu epidemic spread in the Reserves, the shamans conducted their ceremonies 'to cast out the disease' and 'regularly sent cougars [sic] and bears back to hilltop homes they peopled, but they couldn't speak the language of the virus' (*Ravensong* 79). European settlers rejected First Nations healing practices as 'Quackery and superstition' and missionaries actively encouraged people to accept the European health practices.

Maracle presents the comparative concept of the food habits of the First Nations and the settlers. As against the First Nations nature, the settler community prefers fast food to the fresh vegetables available in their yards which effects a drain on their purses which in turn compels the mother to be stingy, when serving food to children: "Aesthetic waste supplanted good sense and thrift in the care of yards, while frantic saving coloured their consumption of food at dinner time. Because they hadn't the good sense to harvest what was in front of them, they had to lighten up on the amount of food. They ate dinner." (*Ravensong* 33)

When a white old woman gave little Stacey a candy, though her mother allowed Stacey to accept it and thanked the white woman, she made the child discard it, when the woman was out of sight, because in the words of the mother such food was only 'poison' though relishing (48). Stacey's mother, who is mentioned as Momma, recalls the words of Grandpa Thomas: 'If we eat like them we'll go crazy like them' (150).

The First Nations world in *Ravensong* is one of peace and contentment. There wasn't any scarcity. But there are signs that natural food sources are exhausting driving them more and more dependent on 'store-bought food.'

Re-establishment of the Trickster, the cultural hero of the First Nations, is intended by First Nations writers, as part of their mission of cultural assertion. The Trickster is central to the First Nations' culture. The Trickster does not offer any teachings but his life is there as lessons for the people. The Trickster can assume both the male and female experience. Basil H. Johnson points out that the Trickster figure is 'the caricatured representation of human nature and character in their many facets' (13).

The First Nations writings further reflect the ritual grounding of their cultures and writers include the 'verbal aspect' (Allen 79) of the ritualistic culture in their writings. These rituals shape and integrate individual lives. Ritual-oriented cultures are built on the assumption that the universe is built around a supernatural force. This ritual grounding is reflected in N. Scott Momaday's novel, *House Made of Dawn* (1968). The novels of James Welsh also draw heavily from the ritualistic culture of the

Indian (Allen 79-80).

Biocentrism is the core of First Nations Culture: "In tribal traditions beings such as certain people and beasts, the sun, the earth and sacred plants, like corn are in a constant state of transformation, and that transformative process engenders the ritual cycle of dying, birth, growth, ripening, dying and rebirth. In the transformation from one state to another, the prior state of condition must cease to exist. It must die." (Allen 80)

Along with human beings, plants, animals and spirits also share the natural space according to the First Nations perceptions. As human beings are in harmony with all occupants of nature, they give offerings to the spirits being treated as the relatives and guardians of human beings in their ethereal existence. Tobacco is the main offering to the spirits. The onslaught of European materialistic culture is causing disruption in the relation of humans with the spirit world. Slipperjack in *Silent Words* is expressing concern over this issue.

The First Nations sing songs for heterogeneous events of their life like war, illness, marriage and death. They have songs to express all emotions like love, sorrow and happiness. The singers maintain a harmony with words, rhythm and melody. In *Ravensong*, Stacey's Momma sings songs when she is desperate. When they saw fire 'caving down' the house of Martha, a member of their community, they faced the inevitable and found solace in singing a song, when their attempt to stop the fire failed. Initiated by Stacey's mother, the others joined her. 'Their bodies rocked together as each villager locked arms with another and they bent their bodies to the song' (120). The song is ritualistic. It purifies them of the pain and sorrow.

The Medicine wheel symbolizes the universe, which is supposed to be binding on the people. It is a circle with horizontal and vertical lines through the centre, which represent the paths. According to their belief system, everything in the universe moves in a circle. Colours have special symbolic significations like green colour symbolizes Mother earth and vegetation, red the animals and humans, blue stands for sky and white symbolizes the Great spirit (Lavalle 149). The colours also signify direction, though with variations with different tribes. Judy Bopp and others maintain that the human self is represented by the Medicine wheel, by projecting its four aspects—the mental, physical, emotional and spiritual. In order to remain healthy, all these four aspects of a person should be in perfect harmony (6).

As in the case of colours, numbers possess special significations. Four stands for the four directions and four medicines. These four medicines are associated with the four directions (Lavalle 150). Because of their smell, these medicines are also called incense. The incense is burned especially for sacred ceremonies to invoke the Great Spirit. Sweet grass is considered a special gift from the Great Spirit to human beings.

Recuperating the culture of the First Nations, practices like offering tobacco, and burning sweet grass are performed by various characters presented in the writings of postcolonial writers. Marianne's Momma in *Sundogs* performs these rites. Slipperjack's Ol Jim offers tobacco to the spirits in his sojourn in the forest (*Silent Words* 97).

The shamans performed a variety of services in the First Nations societies. Other than healing illness, they assisted hunting expeditions, foretold weather, blessed the warriors, communicated with the spirits, prophesied the future.

The First Nations of Canada attributed great significance to dreams. It was believed that dreams are instructions received from the Great Spirit by taking the person to a higher realm. Accordingly, the dictates of the dreams they fulfilled with great piety (Finlay and Sprague 21). The return of Tommy Kelasket to his native home had been predicted by uncle Joe from his dream, and it proved to be true (*Slash* 79). Culleton elaborates on this in her text *Spirit of the White Bison.* The white bison, which had been very special to the First Nations, was once helped by a human being. One day the white bison strolled alone to the spot desiring to meet the man. To his surprise, he saw the man arriving on horseback. Seeing his surprise, the man explained: 'I had a dream you would be here. So I came' (38).

The ceremonies are designed in this pattern. In revitalizing and promoting First Nations culture, ceremonies like the powwow are observed to provide enjoyment and instruction. To further the instruction in their culture, First Nations originated curricula are introduced in their schools.

In the First Nation culture, the Elders are perceived as repositories and transmitters of cultural and spiritual knowledge. Recently they are being called in, to offer their wisdom and guidance gathered from their experience in multifarious levels. They are to be approached with tobacco, and the meeting with them is considered sacred.

April tells how a First Nations Elder woman hailed her. She went with her younger sister Cheryl to a friendship centre, where they met many Elders. 'I knew that Cheryl saw their quiet beauty, their simple wisdom. All I could see were watery eyes, leather brown skin, aged uneducated natives' (*April Raintree* 173). On seeing her, an elderly woman came up to her and took April's hand in hers: "her fingers were swollen at the joints, disfigured, the veins stood out and it took everything I had not to withdraw my hand from hers. . . . I looked at her questioningly but she didn't say anything . . . without speaking a word the woman had imparted her message with her eyes. She had seen something in me that was special, something that was deserving of her respect." (175)

Grandmothers are guides to the youngsters who help them escape the self-hatred, the legacy of colonialism. Campbell's great grandmother, Cheechum, gives her all the moral support she needed, to support and keep together the family after the death of her mother *(Halfbreed*). In the first Nations oral traditions, the experience of one is narrated to others for guidance.

Campbell claims that she is a community worker and she employs her writings to heal her community as well as herself (Hill 46, 56). Slipperjack illustrates in *Silent Words* the First Nations' way of transmitting their wisdom. 'It's Important to remember exactly what is said so that you in turn, when you are an old man, can tell it to a little person like you' (143). When the First Nations individual is treated as the 'other' in the colonial concepts, in the First Nation concept of society, each individual is precious. Slash feels how he and his people are part of a chain formed of generations. 'I saw then that each one of us who faltered was irreplaceable and a loss to all. In that way, I learned how important and how precious my existence was' (203).

The whites perceive that the First Nations are a spiritual people because 'the route to spiritual rebirth is physical labour.' The First Nations do a lot of physical labour and they sustain the white community. The whites are unable to do any physical labour and theirs is a 'parasitic culture.' "Since they rarely work at productive labour that is physical, they cannot conceive of laboriously unraveling their bodily person and discovering that spirit within" (Maracle, *I Am Woman* 149-50).

The Government had been attempting to give the First Nations the image of parasites by putting them on welfare; people like Bobbi Lee's mother 'had a deeply held ethic handed down from both her family and dad's father, that people ought to work' (31). The disempowerment of the chiefs is well in the awareness of Stacey. In the early First Nations societies, the chief was there to see to the problems of the people. Now he has become invisible. The communal nature of the First Nations society is explicit when they are in trouble. Thomas King's *Green Grass, Running Water* projects the solidarity of First Nations in their misfortunes affected by the European ingression of First Nations lands and/ or exploitation of First Nations. When their neighbours were affected by the flu epidemic, Stacey's mother went there with Stacey to help them, instead of isolating the affected house (*Ravensong* 45).

As children were welcomed as a boon, without considering their parentage, there were no orphans. The missionaries who came into contact with these communities could not digest this attitude of the First Nations (Prentice et al 31). When Danny in *Silent Words* ran away from his home, he did not have to starve or suffer, as many First Nations' people were willing to take him in and provide for him. Culleton tries to undermine the Manichean aesthetic through her fictional autobiography. Cheryl, who was proud of her Indian identity, becomes disillusioned at the sight of her father as a gutter creature: 'All my dreams to rebuild the spirit of a once proud nation are destroyed in this instant. I study the pitiful creature in front of me. My father! A gutter creature.' (176).

The ethnocentric spiritual concept of the colonizers rooted in Christianity were diametrically opposite to the spiritual concept of the First Nations and Cheechum laughed at them. Even though Cheechum's beliefs were strongly rooted in the First Nations' spiritual concepts, she could not keep her future generation uninfluenced by the religion of the colonizers. The author's mother was a staunch follower of Christianity (*Halfbreed*). Though Campbell is a Christian, she upholds the spiritual concept of the First Nations and prefers it to the Christian doctrine brought to their land by colonizers. "I have never found peace in a church or in prayer. Perhaps Cheecham had a lot to do with that. Her philosophy was much more practical, soothing and exciting, and in her way I found comfort." (81)

Campbell's Cheechum is representative of the First Nations Elder who communicates to the young generation their spiritual concepts. Slipperjack's character of Jim, a representative of the First Nations Elders, upholds the spiritual concept of the First Nations: 'Contemporary Native literature abounds with characters who are crushed and broken by circumstances and disaster, but very few of them perish. Whatever the damage, contemporary characters, like their traditional trickster relations, rise from their own wreckage to begin again.' (King, *Canadian Fiction Magazine* 8)

Toni Morrison's conviction of the black civilization is applicable to Canadian First Nations civilization in this context: 'This civilization . . . which was underneath the white civilization was there with its own everything. Everything of that civilization was not worth hanging on to. But some of it was and nothing has taken its place while it is being dismantled.' (Ruas 229)

Postcolonial writers project the callous and discriminatory actions of the Christian church in their writings as they presume it as 'participants' in the colonization, and offer resistance to the motives of the church. Campbell believes that the onslaught of Christianity has severely damaged the First Nations culture and religion. She blames Christian church's intrusion in their society for many of their misfortunes. The treatments provided by First Nations' Shamans were perceived to be witchcraft by the Euro-Canadians and often threats of legal action were made by the missionaries and white physicians.

Campbell accuses that the Catholic church was 'the man coming in front of the colonizer . . . the priest had total power in the community. . . . It is still there, but not the kind of influence they had before.' On realizing that they are losing their grip, the church capitalizes on the 'uglier' tactic of adapting First Nations religious ceremonies, targeting to retain the First Nations within their grip, and the priest ends up becoming the shaman in the community (Luz 46-47).

Campbell maintains that the colonizers wielded Christianity as a powerful weapon. It inflicted devastating damage on the First Nations' culture. It constantly attempted to make the First Nations feel ashamed of their faith. It constructed codes for them. Campbell is indignant that even when her people hated the Christian church, they dared not say anything against the church. The priests were not different from the religion they preached.

Campbell remembers with denigration the way the greedy priest selfishly ate up their meagre food. As God and religion were sacred to her mother, she never challenged it. But the priest never showed any respect to what was sacred to them. 'He even dared to take away things from the Indians sun dance pole' (*Halfbreed* 30). The discrimination shown by the priest at the death of her mother adds to her indignation. Even when Campbell's mother had been a devout Christian, the priest refused to hold burial services for her. He made sure that no one dared to ring the church bell for her funeral.

Though the missionaries desired the First Nations embrace Christianity, there was no egalitarian reciprocity. The white people in her neighbourhood discriminated against the Métis and refused any contact with them. Even at Christmas, they don't stop to wish them, but 'drive by all the half-breed houses and drop boxes off at each path' (27). Campbell's visions are moulded by First Nations spirituality and socialism as against the Christian codes.

Slash maintains that the children were disinterested in the catechism of the priest at the nearby church. 'The classes were always boring because we couldn't understand them. If we tried to run away he grabbed us by the ear and twisted hard, so we had to listen' (28-29). Maracle confesses that she started studying the Bible against her wish because of the compulsion of her mother. 'I didn't like it. It was full of unbelievable fantasies' (*Bobbi Lee* 33).

During LaRocque's mother's eight-month illness, no priest or representative of the Christian church visited them or consoled them (*Tides* 112). Campbell upholds that verse 3 to 12 in St. Mathew, chapter 5, is particularly meant to keep the First Nations in subordination. 'Blessed are the poor in spirit for they shall inherit the kingdom of Heaven.' When it was discussed in her class using First Nations as examples, Campbell challenged it and was punished for it (*Halfbreed* 61). The patriarchal codes of Christianity discriminated and subjugated women and First Nations women were doubly marginalized in the colonial world. Stacey resisted the Christian practice of thanking for the food they eat. 'Since she had not been confirmed a catholic [sic] Stacey knew little about their strange customs.' She could not digest the priest 'wanting to know the intimate' secrets of people (*Ravensong* 118).

The European system of education was introduced by the Christian missionaries. The Residential Schools were conceptualized on the assumption that First Nations were inherently uncultured and unhygienic and the schooling imparted to First Nations children was meant to wean them from their cultural practices and to effect cultural homogeneity. The enforced transplantation of First Nations children in the residential schools resulted in the cultural isolation and psychic alienation of the First Nations children. Culleton succeeds in partying this psychic alienation by illustrating the experience of April and her sister Cheryl on the day when the staff of the Children's Aid society came to take them away: 'I clung to my Mom as tight as I could. They wouldn't be able to pull me away from her and then they would leave. I expected Mom to do the same. But she didn't. . . . My mother should have fought with her life to keep us with her. Instead, she had simply handed us over. It didn't make any sense to me.' (8)

The sisters were separated as they were kept in separate foster homes, where they met with the utmost inhuman treatment. As the social workers and teachers were biased, their voice was never listened to which finally leads April to find a louder voice in writing, making it 'heard.' First Nations writer, Rick Tail Feathers, testifies the unsympathetic and racist attitude of the authorities as well as the inhuman disciplinary methods in the residential schools. Observing the resistance offered by Mathew, the First Nations boy, when his parents brought him for his stay in the school, Mrs. Cobb the White matron exclaimed. 'Good lord, what do we have here, a wild savage?' The other members of the staff also joined the laughter that followed the comment (139). Mathew was strictly disallowed the use of his native tongue, Blackfoot at school. 'You must speak English at all times. If you are caught speaking Indian again you will be punished' (139) was the warning given by the matron.

In 'A Long Story,' Beth Brant voices the pain of a First Nations mother, when her children are taken away from her, by the government agents to be educated in the residential schools. The First Nations parents had no say in how to educate their children. They were forcefully taken away and kept at the Residential Schools for years, and when they came off the schools, their language, culture, religion and even their names would be changed. They were made complete strangers to their parents and people (101). The First Nations women's cultural isolation, denial of opportunity to live complete lives, is reflected in Maracle's portrayal of Bertha: 'The efforts of the village woman to nurture her as a keeper of her clan mother of all youth had gone to naught. . . . Motherhood, the recreation of ancient stories that would instruct the young in the laws of her people and encourage good citizenship from even the babies had eluded her' (*Sojourner's Truth* 19-20). It deprived women of their traditional role of teachers and transmitters of culture. The subtext of this Residential School pedagogy is that the church wanted to eliminate the First Nations religious practices and impose Christianity on the First Nations, which they thought was superior.

In the residential schools, First Nations children were exposed to physical and mental abuse and humiliation and discrimination. In order to render the colonized inadequate, the colonizers see themselves as well as the colonized in the light of the power differentials in a colonial situation, which justifies the colonizers' stand (Memmi 95). LaRocque confesses that though she was sorry to leave her parents for the city, each time she boarded the train, she felt the 'tidal waves of changes' taking place between the world of her people and herself (*Tides* 109). At school, the First Nations are conditioned to accept inferiority by the glorification of everything connected with the whites and their supremacy (Adams 15).

The teachers believed that the First Nations were their subordinates and never tolerated the First Nations students doing better than the white students at school. 'Most of the time when I got into a new class the teacher would automatically think I was dumb. I knew that by their remarks' (*Slash* 38).The white students also were not less in degree to the teachers, in humiliating the First Nations students. They teased them about their food, their not having the sophisticated lifestyle like the Euro-Canadians. As Dyer points out: "In the realm of categories, black is always marked as colour (as the team 'coloured' egregiously acknowledges) and is always particularizing; whereas white is not a particularizing quality, because it is everything white is no colour because it is all colours." (44)

Like all the First Nations children of the time Stacey's mother also had gone to the Residential School.' They were all scrubbed clean and deloused. . . . It was such an indignity.' Her mother cried a lot on that humiliation for a week, and the school authorities felt her 'disruptive' and sent her back to her parents (*Ravensong* 107). The White system of disciplining was most shocking to First Nations, especially at residential schools. There were rules for everything and if you failed to follow any of the rules, you were punished which was traumatic to the First Nations children who were living in a free society, without any kind of restrictions. Jeannette Armstrong lashes against this policy and calls this condition totalitarianism: "Our children for generations were seized from our communities and homes and placed in indoctrination camps until our language, our religions, our customs, our values and our societal structures almost disappeared. This was the residential school experience. Arising out of the siege conditions of this nightmare time what is commonly referred to as the 'social problems' of the Native people emerged. Homes and communities without children had nothing to work for or live for." (*Disempowerment* 207)

The undergirding spirit of the First Nations educational system is to develop a positive self-image among the First Nations people. Elders are to ensure the standard and perfection of the First Nations languages taught in the First Nations schools.

Maracle is strongly against the European practice of disciplining students. When asked about the First Nations run En'Owkin school she says: "We try to hothouse the students' own skills to build what's in their own selves. It's the way Native people teach and learn. My parents, my mother anyway encouraged me to realize myself rather than battering me with useless instructions about don't touch this, and sit at the table, and be still, and don't talk too much. I was given choices at a very early age, either reading or writing." (Williamson 175)

English the imperialist language proved to be 'basic to white supremacy and inferiorization' (Adam 134). As Michal Stevenson points out colonialism's project 'was, and still is to lay waste a people and destroy their culture in order to undermine the integrity of their existence and appropriate their riches.' This is attained through 'total war' employing race and language in constructing negative image to justify the annihilation of First Nations 'Language becomes basis for the forming of national identity and for providing the state with an organizing ideology whose racist imperialist concepts 'become institutionalized as the democratic nation state' where the First Nations is othered (28).

Kenyan writer Ngugi maintained that language was 'the most important vehicle through which power fascinated and held the soul prisoner' (*Decolonizing the Mind* 9). When language was manipulated to fix the history of the empire, the colonized exploited the potential of language in their counter discursive writings. Many postcolonial writers feel uncomfortable with

English, as it is language of the colonizer. Joy Harjo calls it 'the enemy's language' and Emma LaRocque believes that since it is the 'enemy's language' it ought to be transformed. Its 'stinging layers of racism and sexism must be peeled away before it can be fully enjoyed.' (Preface, *Writing the Circle*, xx, xxvi).

The language of many of the former colonies are variations of English. Colonization left the Caribbean a rootless nation because of its population of diverse races from Africa, East India and Europe. It hasn't got a common history, culture or language. Caribbean writer Jean D'Costa illustrates the dilemma facing the writers: "The [Caribbean] writer operates within a poly dialectal continuum (sic) with a Creole base. His medium, written language belongs to the sphere of standardized language which exerts a pressure within his own language community while embracing the wide audience of international Standard English.

He is forced to 'evolve a literary dialect' that would be acceptable to his readers inside and outside the nation (qtd. Deena 103). A variety of languages is incorporated into English, in the postcolonial writings, abrogating the privileged status of English. By imposing anglicized names to persons and places, the colonizers' supremacy is imposed on them, erasing traces of First Nations language and culture. Campbell articulates her fear of being silenced by the loss of language in her *Book of Jessica* (1989): "I'd feel the conqueror, the oppressor making me use his language, and I know I'd never use it as well as him and I'd feel so powerless, and think, 'They stole everything, and now we can't just speak anymore, the old language is almost gone and we don't know the new language well enough to help each other, heal each other. . . . We're just hanging here in the middle." (73)

Structures are enforced on the colonial writers by the impostors' language that cripples the expression of the First Nations experience which Raja Rao rightly expresses in the author's 'Foreword' to *Kanthapura* (1938); "One has to convey in a language that is not one's own the spirit that is one's own . . . we cannot write like the English. We should not. . . . Our method of expression therefore has to be a dialect which will someday prove to be as distinctive and colourful as the Irish or the American. Time alone will justify it." (vii) But heterogeneous linguistic sources are exploited by colonists to unfold their colonial experience. Salman Rushdie stresses the need for the decolonization of language (8).

Postcolonial writers explore the possible impacts of these linguistic power differentials, through their characters. Baba in Anita Desai's *Clear Light of Day* (1980), Sarah in Brian Friel's *Translation* (1984) and Okonkwo in Chinua Achebe's *Things Fall Apart* (1958) experience problem of articulation, which is represented as a characteristic of the fragmentation created by the divergent terrains of linguistic systems in their society. This linguistic gap created by the imposition of English language left the new generation devoid of the nuances to grasp the orator of the old. The old could neither communicate in English nor teach their language to the new generation as they were taken away from homes at a very early age.

The divergent signifying system added to the silencing of the writer Campbell. She was forbidden from using her First Nations tongue at school. Because of her poor skill in the English language, she kept silent for fear of ridicule. At home, her people knew only the vernacular and were proud of it. So she could not attempt speaking English at home. She argues for a plural language that is not subordinate to English. She calls this language 'village English' and claims that it is more like oral tradition 'in which she could express much better' (Luz 49). During a conversation with Barbara Carey, Nourbese Philip declares that working in English is like coming to terms with an abusive parent (Carey 19). Bell hooks challenges the hegemony of the English language by negating its semantic codes.

Campbell Hale confesses that linguistic alienation necessitates the adaptation of the English language according to their culture and traditions (Introduction, Cecelia Capture). Ashcroft, Griffiths and Tiffin predicated that in order to jettison colonial values created by English, postcolonial writers subvert standard English syntax by introducing untranslatable words from regional language and creolizing obscure standard English terms thus creating new 'Englishes.'

The new Englishes developed in the colonized nation's claim an identity of its own that is unbridgeable to the Standard English of the centre, rejecting the colonial values, established by the English of the colonizer.

Many writers like Maria Campbell and Beatrice Culleton have reclaimed their First Nations names instead of the Europeanized Christian names and the anglicized version of the names in First Nations tongues. Kenyan writer James Ngugi is now known by his Native name Ngugi wa Thiong'o. Many of the historic First Nations' characters also are mentioned by their First Nations names, by the resistance writers, subverting the status of English.

The prospect of first-person narration is explored by these writers to 'suppress the role of language in the construction of the subject, and its own role in the interpellation of the subject, and to present the individual as a free, unified, autonomous subjectivity' (Belsey 67). The construction of the 'I' effects a shift from the constructed 'other' image, thus resisting the subversive tactics of the colonizer. These writings hold out hope to the many Canadian First Nations who suffer from an 'identity crisis' (New 172).

In decolonizing the English language, the Blacks face a complicated situation when English is the colonizer's language, it is their mother tongue too. When the middle and the upper classes in the lower echelons of the community speak English, which Nourbese Philip refers to as Caribbean demotic. It is said as 'Patois' or 'bad English.' Luce Irigaray contends that to the Black women writers, primacy is to politics of language and the role of signifying system in society:

> Through their writings they illuminate the latent contradictions in seemingly coherent systems of thought, indicating possibilities in nothingness, absence, marginalization, and repression, and they celebrate plurality and difference. In doing so they prompt their readers to 'reinterpret the whole relationship between the subject and discourse, the subject and the world, the subject and the cosmic, the microcosmic and the macrocosmic.' (119)

To dismantle the English language from its pedestal and to project her affiliation to her mother tongue, Campbell installs many signifiers from her Cree tongue in *Halfbreed* as well as in *The Book of Jessica*. This hybridization of language is again employed in her children's book *Little Badger and the Fire Spirit* (1980). Campbell confesses the convergence of multiple languages in her writings: 'I grew upon Shakespeare, Sir Walter Scott and Longfellow' (*Halfbreed* 13).

By mixing vernacular with English, Campbell feels that she could keep close to her tradition and community—a plural language that is not subordinate to English. She calls this language 'Village English' and claims that it is more like 'Oral tradition' in which she could 'express much better' (Lutz 49). Campbell's *Road Allowance People* (1995) is written in this 'broken' or 'Village English.' The Métis identity further constituted linguistic pluralism as she postulates, 'we spoke a language completely different from the other. We were a combination of everything: hunters, trappers and ak-ee-top (pretend) farmers' (*Halfbreed* 25). Maracle employs words from First Nations language in *Sundogs*. The title word Sundogs in First Nations language means, 'impossible images reflected under extraordinary circumstances' (185). The characters do not bother to follow the semantics of the English language in *Ravensong*. By employing plural voice, these writers effect the displacement of the English language. Along with the imposition of constraints on First Nations language, Europeans attempted to subvert First Nations literature by imposing their literary codes. The written word was the true medium to the Europeans, which left the oral tradition of the First Nations unacknowledged. The colonial subjects had been constrained and conditioned by the study of the canonical texts in class rooms inculcating the culture and practices of the Europeans, undermining the exigencies of the First Nations context. The European genre distinctions began to be applied on literary output, sweeping aside the First Nations orality, as it is not scribal. Literary output enters the fold of literature only if it fits into the genre distinction of the Europeans. Frederic Jameson refutes the European concept by the assertion: 'Genres are essentially literary institutions [sic] or social contracts between a writer and a specific public whose function is to specify the proper use of particular cultural artifact' (106). The politics of the canon/ genre was resisted by the First Nations writers, by making visible an alternate aesthetic that had remained marginalized. This alternate aesthetic attempts to dismantle the power structures of the canonical texts of the imperial topologies. Writers like Arnold Krupat and Louis Owens challenge the traditions of valuing non-western writings in western theoretical perspective. Nancy Hartsock feels that the minorities had been marginalized by the transcendental voice of universalizing theory (*Cultural Critique* 204). The First Nations literatures had been appropriated by the European translation and reinterpretation. Lee Maracle predicates the problem: 'Postcolonialism presumes we have resolved the colonial condition, at least in the field of literature. Even here we are still a classical colony. Our words, our sense and use of language are not judged by the standards set by the poetry and stories we create. They are judged by the standards set by others' (*Postcolonial Imagination* 13). In spite of the stifling imposed on the canonical literary world, the First Nations writers went on writing profusely, mostly their personal experiences in the political realm. Their orality remains a distinctive marker or First Nations discourse. First Nations autobiographical discourse is a resistance tactic as autobiography in the western concept is ego-centric narration. In First Nations autobiographical texts, diffusion of multiple voices and identities are signalized, as literature in First Nations societies was communal in nature. The life writing by these writers dismisses the European genre of autobiography resisting the hegemony of the genres of dominant discourses. Exploiting its 'oppositional potential' (Krupat 35), First Nations writers appropriate the autobiographical genre constituting its difference. Further the referential dimension of autobiography has become increasingly delusive since Roland Barthes' argument of *The Death of the Author* (1968) and Michael Foucault's declaration of *What is an Author?* (1977). Post-Saussurian deconstructionist criticism has subverted the authenticity and authority of autobiography. Penny Petrone observes: 'Resurgence of cultural and religious values has made these writers realize that they are heirs to a wealth of traditional oral literature upon which they can look for inspiration and direction.' (182)

Scholars of America are arguing for the inclusion of the oral literature of the First Nations to be included as literature of the First Nations to be included as literature. As in every other matter, the First Nations consider their literary output the product of the community. They do not claim it as individual contribution. Saskatchewan writer Beth Cuthand observes: Often when we are writing, it is not our words that are coming. The grandmothers and grandfathers come and write through us. There have been instances where I've written a poem or a short story and looked at it after it was written and said to myself, 'I don't quite understand this' and then it would take may be five years to come to an understanding of the content. (53)

Postcolonial writers destabilize the colonial assumptions by articulating re-workings of canonical texts and thus offer a counter discourse decanting the significations of imperialist topologies. Undermining settler mythologies and adventure stories is part of the arsenal of postcolonial writers against the European canon. Rewiring the much-orchestrated exploration tales of the Europeans, the role and value of the explorer/ hero is dismantled and he is presented from the First Nations perspective. Aboriginal writer Mudrooroo Noongar (Colin Johnson) conceptualizes the First Nations perspective of colonization through *Dr. Wooreddy's Prescription for Enduring the Ending of the World and Master of the Ghost Dreaming* (1987).

The publishing world proved to be in collusion with the white forces to discriminate the First Nations women writers by turning down their attempts to get their works published. They overcame this hurdle by establishing publishing houses like Theytus publications, Pemmican publications, write-on press publishers, Fifth House publishers etc. The conventional European practice is to mention the publishing house who produce the book, along with the title of the book and the writer's signature. W.H. New observes that in Maracle's' I am Woman no publisher is mentioned on the title page and on the next page 'write on publishers 1988' is mentioned. Write on press publisher had not been there as an established publisher. Here Maracle is pursuing the First Nations convention (204). When Maralce expresses her debt to the colonized peoples of the world all over, for the publication of her book, Armstrong expresses her resistance to European convention by publishing her book through a First Nations owned publishing house, 'Theytus Books.' Merlene Nourbese Philip points out that her award-winning novel *Harriet's Daughter* (1989) had been returned by the publishers marking 'Not marketable' (*Globe and Mail* 7).

Even though Maracle acknowledges that academic work on postcolonialism and literature is necessary, as 'in the real-world colonialism is our condition' (*Postcolonial Imagination* 13). Instead of pursuing the European pattern of dividing a prose work into chapters, Marchessault marks the divisions of her trilogy as songs Kristjana Gunner's work The Prowler isn't organized in chapters but in very small numbered fragments. Thomas King marks the development of his narration of Green Grass, Running Water by the names of directions and the colours associated with them. Maracle's *I Am Woman*, had been rejected by a publishing house since it doesn't comply with the European genre distinction (Williamson 173).

Resistance to European genre distinctions is discernible in the Australian Aboriginal writer Sally Morgan. Morgan traces the ancestry of an Aboriginal family to the oral sources, highlighting the First Nations Oral traditions, establishing a space for the First Nations in the white dominated world in *My Place* (1987). Thus as Gilbert and Tompkins observe, 'Critiques of postcolonialism are frequently responses to arguments based primarily on attempts to homogenize texts, histories and cultures.' (4)

Resistance in Drama and Poetry

> I'd feel the conqueror, the oppressor, making me use his language, and I know I'd never use it as well as him and I'd feel powerless, and think, 'They stole everything and now we can't just speak any more, the old language is almost gone and we don't know the new language well enough to help each other, heal each other . . . we're just hanging there in the middle (Linda Griffiths and Maria Campbell, *The Book of Jessica*, 73)

Though drama is one of the earliest forms of literature, it developed only very recently in the Canadian First Nations society. The Society for the Re-establishment of the Trickster helped a great deal in the development of First Nations drama. The First Nations stage performance tradition is not free from the influence of French and English Drama.

The establishment of the various theatres of drama like the Red Roots Theatre Group, in Winnipeg, the De-ba-jeh-mu-jug Theatre Group in Manitoulin island, Ontario, Native Earth Performing Arts Theatre Passe Muraille in Toronto, the Upisasik Theater of Ile-a-la-Cross, Saskatchewan are some of the theatre companies that act as catalysts in the development of First Nations drama. Men dominated the field of First Nations drama and the women dramatists in Canada are few in number. Why it happened like that is a problem to be discussed. The subordinate status of women in society may be a reason for women to keep away from this sphere.

Since theatre practitioners have immense opportunities to intervene explicitly in the social and political organizations and stage critiques of their structures, multiplicity of strategies were employed by First Nations dramatists to encounter the dissolution of the signifiers of the First Nations. The playwrights of the suppressed peoples of the empire began exploiting stage space to implicate their displacement and disempowerment consequent to colonial expansions of the Europeans. As Ashcroft and others maintain, 'the dialectic of space and displacement' (*Empire Writes Back* 9) became a key issue in postcolonial drama. The meagre output by First Nations women dramatists necessitates the inclusion of male writers to exemplify the counter discursive tactics in stage performance.

The notable women writers who have found a niche in this sphere are Maria Campbell, Monique Mojica, Yvette Nolan and Margo Kane. In *The Book of Jessica: A Theatrical Transformation* (1989), Maria Campbell explores the issue of the appropriation of First Nations women and culture and the sensitivities of a people. In this, Campbell collaborates with a non-First Nations actress Linda Griffiths. It suggests the problems faced by an actor of one culture to present the experiences of a person of another culture. Marlene Nourbese Philip in her one act play 'Coups and Calypso' stresses the racialization problematic of the world: 'Indian should marry Indian and African marry African, and White marry White. Dove and Corbeau should never mate although both a dem is [sic] bird' (12).

The traumatic experience of a First Nations girl in the Residential School is thematized by the Cree writer Shirley Cheechoo. She experiments with the technique of drama. Instead of the dialogic form, this drama is in the form of a monologue. The protagonist, a schoolgirl named Shirley, is found locked up in a room when the play begins. She talks to the audience and the objects that she sees before her and tells of her experience revealing the horrors of the Residential School system.

Canadian First Nations male writer Drew Hayden Taylor thematizes the same topic and satirizes the Canadian government's education policy on the First nations in *Education is Our Right* (1990). The Residential school, meant to acculturate the

First Nations, is critiqued by the playwright. The government maintained double standards on the First Nations and Euro-Canadian students. The play is a downright critique of the policies of the DIA. An exegesis of the pain experienced by the First Nations families during the period of the Residential School system is dealt with by Hayden Taylor in *Someday* (1993). Anne, the First Nations mother waits, for a lifetime for the return of her first-born child Grace, who had been taken away from her by the Children's Aid Society. The child grew up unattached to its biological parents and their culture. The play ends with the grown-up woman Grace, now called Janice, leaving, promising to return to her mother someday. In *Only Drunks and Children Tell the Truth* (1996) written as sequel to *Someday*, we find Janice (Grace) hating her biological mother. She had imposed the image that the biological mother was alcoholic like the other lost women of Reserves and believed that due to this, she was brought up by White adopted parents. She hated that fate and developed a hatred for her mother. Towards the end of the play, Janice comes to her mother's grave to 'seek forgiveness' (76) from her. She was heavily drunk and she pours out the weight in her heart that had been unbearable to her. She confesses, 'all I wanted was evidence, proof to justify my anger.' But on seeing her, 'everything [she] had wanted to believe was gone.' Because her mother did not suit the image she had constructed which 'made' her 'ever more anger.' Now she prays for forgiveness (77).

In *Prince Pocahontas and the Blue Sports* (1990), Monique Mojica attempts to establish a space for the First Nations women, by exposing the European imposed paradigms on the First nations women juxtaposing the colonial constructs with contemporary reality. She contests the negative definitions on the First Nations women. Deconstructing the assigned semiotic field of the First Nations woman, she counters their White defined stereotypical identities by presenting representatives of contemporary Indian society. *The Moonlodge* (1990) by Margo Cane again is an attempt with the same motive.

David Diamond and others' 'No Xya' (1990) reclaim First Nations culture and practices. Incorporating First Nations rituals, it props up the First Nations land claims against the provincial government. Among the North Americas tribes there is a practice of invoking the Gods for protection of the actors by drawing a sacred circle. Maria Campbell suggests the need for this kind of protection to the actors by 'doing the circle every morning and every night' while beginning and ending rehearsals (Griffiths and Campbell 40).

A similar practice is pursued among certain East Indian stage performances, especially of the Hindus. They commenced the performance with a 'Rangapooja' or prayer with lighted traditional lamps called 'Nilavilakku.' Devotional rites like propitiating the God Ganesha—'Ganesha Pooja'—to avoid obstacles also is in existence.

The Eurocentric theatre practices had perpetuated the paradigmatic status of Shakespeare which provokes the Australian writer Penny Gay to raise the question: 'How can one aspire to write plays when Shakespeare has already, incontrovertibly written the greatest dramas in the English language?' (204). Gayatri Spivak has termed this moulding of dramatic practices on received performance traditions as the 'epistemic violence' of colonialism (Critical Inquiry 251). The status of Shakespeare as the paradigm of dramatic art is challenged by indigenous writers by the rendition of Shakespeare texts with the fusion of indigenous elements. Counter-discursive strategies are attempted on canonical texts to deconstruct the cultural significations of the imperial legacy and colonial conditioning, which Helen Tiffin terms 'canonical counter discourse' (*Kunapipi* 22). Though dismantling the canonical assumptions, the counter-discursive enunciation retains many of the significations of the canonical texts. Among counter-discursively reworked texts, Shakespeare's plays are the most targeted ones. The reworking of *The Tempest* encodes the colonial resistance of European imperialism, by the refiguration of the character Caliban as a representative of the resisting colonized (Gilbert and Tomkins 19).

The reworking of The Tempest was initiated by the publication of O. Mannoni's *Prospero and Caliban: The Psychology of Colonization* (1950) and Fanon's *Black Skin, White Masks* (1952). The Prospero/ Caliban relationship was reworked in the light of postcolonialism as the relationship of the colonizer/ colonized. To the Third world writers, Caliban is the representative of the colonized Third World Nations, subjugated by the imperial power.

In 1989, Skylight Theatres of Toronto demonstrated a counter-discursive performance of The Tempest by a rendition of Caliban and Ariel represented as First Nations of Canada. First Nations themes were integrated into the character of Ariel as Raven, the Trickster, who is the cultural hero of the Indians. Traditional cultural elements like the potlatch were incorporated into the presentation, where the Europeans were presented as 'Visitors from hell' whose presence ended up in the death of the lives and culture of the First Nations (Gilbert and Tompkins 26).

The incorporation of regional ritual in association with cultural practices in postcolonial drama are sites of resistance, attempts to assert their culture, performed according to the specificities of the regional theatre, instead of pursuing the complex representational matrix of the colonizer. Rituals stand out as signifiers of cultural difference. It further revitalizes the community by reviving their belief system and re-establishing their lost culture, history and tradition. Further postcolonial drama seeks to disengage themselves from the conventions of the imperial centre (Gilbert and Tompkins 55).

As a master narrative that had been widely used to justify colonial strategies, the Bible is targeted for counter discourse. The re-workings of the Biblical myths were meant to expose the hegemonic concepts of European culture and the motivations of the colonizing Whites in their dealing with the First Nations. Metis writer Yvette Nolan challenges the racial biases of Christianity through the play 'Job's Wife or the Delivery of Grace.' The writer challenges the Christian practice of confession for absolution:

> What odd customs you have. Instead of apologizing to the one you have wronged and making restitution to that one, you go into a little box and whisper your mistakes to someone who doesn't know you and doesn't care about what you've done, and he tells you that it's all right. No wonder you have such a hard time getting on in this world; you make it so hard for yourselves. . . . Do you feel cleansed when you come out of that little box? (30)

This resistance is discernible in the dramatic presentation in Australian writers. Australian Aboriginal writer Jack Davis in his play In Our Town (1990) lashes at Christian missionaries: 'Wetjala cunning fellow alright. When they come [sic] here they had the Bible and we had the land, [now] they've got the land and we've got the Bible' (44).

Drew Hayden Taylor suggests that in their First Nations life of contentment, 'they did not have complicated problems' as problems are the result of man's artificial life (*Toronto at Dreamers Rock* 46-47). When a race discards its culture and way of life, they cannot 'fit in' (47) and problems erupt. That is what the First Nations are experiencing now.

In Thompson Highway's *Dry Lips Oughta Move to Kapuskasing* (1989), the First Nations youth Dickie Bird's rape of a First Nations woman Patsy, performed holding a crucifix, is suggestive of Christianity's assault on First Nations' space, which is blamed for the schism among the First Nations. The playwright further projects the negative impact of Christianity and colonization on First Nations life. To Spooky Lacroix's challenges on the power of First Nations medicine people, Simon Starblanket points out that the power of the medicine people are debilitated by the acculturation process initiated by the medical establishment and Christian Church, together with the neglect and marginalization of Christian fanatics like Spooky (346). He further challenges the power of Christianity: "Why can't you and that thing (pointing to the Bible) and all it stands for cure your nephew's madness as you call it? . . . What has this [the Bible] done to cure the madness of the community and communities across the country. . . . Why didn't 'the lord,' as you call him, come to your sister's rescue at that bar seventeen years ago" (346).

Starblanket believes that to the First Nations, survival lies in the revival and retention of First Nations ways. Highway utilizes *The Rez Sisters* (1986) to point out the experiences of seven sisters of a First Nations family, their dislocation and/ or displacement in the realm of Canadian society in the 1960s, underlining the racial subtext of Christianity and its denial on First Nations life. Highway upholds the First Nations religion and culture reviving the mythical figures like Nanabush undermining the Christian gods.

Language is rendered as a tool in the imperialist tactics of the Europeans. In order to control the colonial subjects, the colonizers endeavoured to stifle the First Nations' languages and impose English, the imperialists' language. Regardless of the exigencies of the colonial subject, the inculcation of English language and literature was enforced as part of the agenda of 'civilizing' them. George Ryga exposes the stupidity of this manoeuvre in his *Ecstasy of Rita Joe* (1967) through the title character who is forced to learn Wordsworth's poem. The context remains incomprehensible to the First Nations girl, however hard the teacher tries. The introduction of the other communicative systems like song and music in stage performances is part of the attempt to dismantle English from its pedestal (Ashcroft 117). The loss of language effects the loss of culture, history and connections with geographical space. As Ashcroft and others point out, languages' 'system of values—its suppositions, its geography, its concept of history, of difference, its myriad gradations of distinction become the system upon which social, economic and political discourses are grounded' (*Postcolonial Studies* 283). By suppressing their language, the First Nations' sense of autonomy and dignity is erased by the colonizers. Campbell expresses concern at the hegemonic oppression by the English Language. "I'd feel the conqueror, the oppressor, making me use his language, and I know I'd never use it as well as him and I'd feel so powerless and think, 'They stole everything and now we can't just speak any more, the old language is almost gone and we don't know the new language well enough to help each other, heal each other . . . we're just hanging there in the middle" (*The Book of Jessica* 73).

The absence of scriptoriality led to the disempowerment of many First Nations languages. The authority of scriptorial English language is challenged by the reinstallation of oral discourses. Thomson Highway points out the multivalent significations of employing the Cree language in his play. The tactic revives the Cree language as well as culture. Non-Cree speakers are eschewed out of the world of the characters. 'When you speak Cree you laugh constantly' (*Border Crossings* 27). Highway does not follow the European standards of characterization.

Characters with speech impediments are cast in *The Rez Sisters* and *Dry Lips*. Their muteness is a symbol of linguistic suppression effected by imperialism. Dickie Bird in *Dry Lips* writes his ideas out due to this handicap. Dickie Bird's use of English and Cree represents the First Nations 'forked tongue' in the colonial world. His speaking and singing in his native Cree consequent to his vision of his mother symbolically suggests the reclamation of his mother tongue. Daniel David Moses writes in Cree with English interpretations in his 'Almighty voice and His wife.' There are writers who confine to English in writing their plays. Agnes Grant maintains that it is suggestive of their loss of language (109).

Shakespeare's Caliban is a symbolic rendition of the passivity of the colonized as silent in imperial representation. In postcolonial plays, presentation of silence proves to be a more eloquent mode of resistance to the imperial impositions. Caliban subverts Prospero's role as teacher. The colonized do not gain anything positive from the impostors' language, as language is culture bound, which is reflected in his words to Prospero: 'you taught me language and my profit in it/ Is, I know how to curse (*Tempest* I.ii 363-64).

First Nations writers' excavation of the orality of First Nations' languages is to rebut the accredited notion that high-flown language as in Shakespearean tragedies is appreciated in plays. The First Nations language brought the stages close to people, eventually displacing the colonizers' language. Highway's *Dry Lips* thus got unprecedented acclaim in the playhouses and critical circles. In Lieu of this assumption, Australian writer Alex Buzo employs vernacular language in his play 'Norm and Ahmed' (1973). To effect a postcolonial discourse of alterity, traditional forms of gestures and mime are employed to express linguistic autonomy by way of political resistance. As Ashcroft, Griffith and Tiffin contend, the application of First Nations' languages and other theatrical signifiers "localizes and attracts value away from a British 'norm,' eventually displacing the hegemonic centrality of the idea of 'norm' itself" (*Empire Writes Back* 37)

This is the causation of French writer Michael Tremblay's insistence that his plays be presented only in French in his province Quebec. Though he allowed translation in other Canadian languages, the translation to English was allowed only later. It is a rebuttal of the authority of the English language and its universality.

Kenyan writer Ngugi's eschewal to write in English language and his preference of Native Gikuyu is to resist the privileged status of English over other languages of the empire. Drew Hayden Taylor extensively applies the First Nations language to

Ojibway in the play *Bootlegger Blues* (1991). He presents in the play the content family life of the First Nations as against that of the Whites. In Hayden Taylor's *Only Drunks and Children Tell the Truth*, the character Tonto represents the First Nations social world. Bard who was brought up as a First Nations woman takes up the responsibility of holding the family together whereas her sister Janice who was brought up in the European society lives independently. She gives priority to her personal interests only, as against the First Nations way. The two sisters represent the contrast between the European and the First Nations ways of life.

Highway's *The Rez Sisters* focuses on the displacement and dislocation experienced by First Nations women in the divergent terrains of their existence consequent to colonization. Highway's women characters bolstered by Nanabush, the cultural hero of the First Nations, fight against the imperialist patriarchal canons, demonstrating the subversion of First Nations values.

The subversion of the racial subtext in the body politik in colonial signification is another strategy exploited by the resistance writers in their process of cultural decolonization. Australian First Nations writer Jack Davis's 'Kullark' (1982) is an attempt to subvert the White construct of superiority by presenting the First Nations as finding the appearance of Europeans as unnatural. The play illustrates the inhumanity of the Europeans who skin a First Nations man for museumising it for its tribal marks. Downplaying the White man's concept of his superiority due to complexion, Drew Hayden Taylor asks in the play *Toronto at Dreamers Rocks*: 'Why is he [White man] White? Is he not well? (39). The writer also hints at the fact that the white man has no right here as he came from another land.

Non-White characters were presented on stage only to elicit laughter with a comic representation of their culture and costumes. Serious roles were meant for Whites only. Even when the characters are non-whites like Shakespeare's Othello, the performance is done by White actors (Goldie 5). Postcolonial drama steps beyond this prescribed space and represents First Nations characters and actors highlighting their culture and dress codes. First Nations writer David Diamond's 'No Xyz' signifies this.

In colonial discourse, 'the body is the strategic target of system of codification, supervision and constraint' (Grosz 64). Its signification is reviewed in the recuperative process of colonized subjects. Elleke Boehmer maintains: "In colonial representation, exclusion or suppression can often literally be seen as 'embodied.' From the point of view of the colonizer specifically, fears and curiosities, sublimated fascinations with the strange or the 'primitive' are expressed in concrete physical and anatomical images. . . . The other is cast as corporeal, carnal, untamed, instinctual, raw, and therefore also open to mastery, available for use, for husbandry, for numbering, branding, cataloguing, description or possession" (269).

Postcolonial feminist drama finds in the female corporeal signifiers sites for decolonization. Feminist writer Peggy Phelan argues: 'In excessively marking the boundaries of the woman's body, in order to make it thoroughly visible, patriarchal culture subjects it to legal artistic and psychic surveillance. This in turn, reinforces the idea that she is her body' (30).

The colonizer as well as the colonized patriarchy had established a link between woman and the land. Rape is employed as signifier of the colonizers violation/ ingression of unoccupied space. Ryga delineates the rape of his central character by three white men as an assault on First Nations territory and culture. Rita Joe becomes the symbol of First Nations culture assaulted and subordinated by the invaders. In *Rez Sisters*, Highway treats rape as the occupation of female space and gender subordination as well as a symbol of the violation of First Nations culture and land. Zhaboonigan, the mentally disabled First Nations girl lacks understanding of the sexual violence done on her by a gang of White boys as her agonizing experience had been absorbed by the Trickster who has the experience of both the sexes.

As gender designates an aspect of marginality on colonial relationships, several plays articulated gender roles in colonial configurations, attempting opportunities for self-definition for women in the postcolonial world. In Canadian playwright Judith Thompson, pregnancy symbolizes evil and disease (*The Other Side of the Dark*). In J. Shearer's *Catherine* (1977), the traditional notion that pregnancy is the fruition of female body is subverted and it is denigrated as a pathological disorder (Gilbert and Tompkins 220).

The female body was commodified in the slave trade for the purposes of their breeding capacities (*Ibid.* 216). Dennis Scots' 'An Eco in the Bone' (*Play for Today*) presents an effective delineation of the exploitation of the female body for its reproductive capacities. In one scene where the setting is an early 19th century slave market, a Black agent 'lists' the 'attributes' of the 'anatomy' of two female slaves, exhibited as 'merchandise' before a trader whereas the male slave's attribute is not his anatomy (*Ibid.* 216).

First Nations forms of documentation of events is put into requisition in dismissing the falsification in imperial history. The Indian playwright Utpal Dutt undermines the presumptions of White superiority applying oral narrative traditions in recounting the rising against colonial government in his *The Great Rebellion 1857* (1973). The play dislodges the imperial history and galvanizes the spirit of the people to establish their authority in imperial India.

Postcolonial theatres exploit theatre practices as a critique of the political structure that had been imposing its hegemonic approach in subjugating the people of the colonial world, offering resistance through language, theme and performance techniques. Australian aboriginal writer Louis Naura through *Inside the island* (1980) and *Sunrise* (1983) charts his visions of the termination of imperial control and the reinstallation of a more enabling and ecofriendly First Nations system of social order.

Political intervention often curtails theatrical freedom by censorship, banning the play and even imprisonment to the playwrights as in the case of Ngugi wa Thiong'o in Kenya. However in the wake of the theory of deconstruction, the white manifestations of their hegemony are crumbling and the cultural isolation imposed on the First Nations writers is being lifted. The recent movements like Marxism, Feminism and Ecological movement have resulted in the resurgence of the First Nations voice speaking against centuries of suppression and subjugation.

> And all her thoughts are with the days gone by
> Ere might's injustice banished from their lands
> Her people that today unheeded lie
> Like the dead husks that rustler though her hands.
> (Pauline Johnson, 'The Corn Husker,' ed. Moses and Goldie 32)

As First Nations dramatists overtly critiqued imperialism's impositions, First Nations resistance poets mostly problematized an ecofeminist perspective of the colonial situation. They emphasized the eccentric structure of the social and political concepts. Jeannette Armstrong effectively wielded her pen for the empowerment of First Nations and attempted all genres of writing for the purpose. The exploration of varying techniques in poetry itself offers resistance to the genre distinctions of the Europeans. Armstrong's ideology is rooted in the First Nations oral traditions, concept of ecology and culture. As in the First Nations, tradition, poetry is to be orally transmitted, to be sung or performed on stage, it should adhere to rhythmic pattern. Armstrong divulges this ideology and had even performed some of her poems on stage, to be 'within the circle' (Tallon 288).

Breath Tracks (1991), Armstrong's collection of poems, is divided into four parts. Here, land is symbolized as the grandmother in the First Part of the poem entitled 'From the Landscape of the grandmother,' suggesting human beings' undetectable relation to it. Land is a binding force with its children. The

First Nations never owned the land. They only made a discretionary use of it, keeping in view the seventh generation. They believed that everything on land is to be preserved for posterity.

Armstrong's poems serve as vehicles for her political ideology of the resistance of colonial subjugation of First Nations. The technique of juxtaposition is employed in 'High Bracken mountain' (96) to expose the superficial attitude of the White colonizers. The poem 'Blood' (16-17) traces the descent of the community, the resilience and unity of the people through thick and thin, the challenges they have to face due to the present-day predicament in view of their posterity, are implied. The oral tradition of the First Nations had been the binding force in them in resisting the onslaught of colonization:

> Voice of continuance
> Countless sound shaping which roll
> Over millions of tongues
> To reach me. (17)

In the poem 'Keepers Words' Armstrong celebrates the power of the word, the First Nations language, which withstood the onslaught of colonization.

> There will be now new words
> In man-designs to break up what is sacred and
> Leave forget in its place
> We are keepers we must not change. (*Breath Tracks* 91).

The contribution of oral tradition in the survival of First Nation culture thought centuries of suppression and the danger in discarding one's own language is thematized by Armstrong in 'Threads of old Memory' (*Breath Tracks* 58) when Armstrong directly instructs the readers against the danger of discarding one's own language. Claire Harris urges her child to struggle for the dismantling of English and the recuperation of their lost First Nations tongue in 'Drawing Down Daughter' (1992).

The stifling of First Nations' language was intended at the

European schools to suppress the culture of the First Nations. This stifling of language in the young generation results in the discarding of the culture of the First nations by their young people. Mary Augusta Tappage bewails that after her education at the Mission school, she experienced the schism between her people and herself. She lost her language 'Shuswap' which had been wrenched from her at school. She failed to understand her people, as her people knew only their native tongue (Moses and Goldie 39).

Tappage remembers how the Lillooet Indians go to the north to work in the 'Goldfields up by Baskerville.' They work from dawn to dusk. Though the poet watches 'them passing,' she 'couldn't ask them where they go' as their language is incomprehensible to her. Now that she knows only English, she could not use that with her people (*Ibid.* 39-40).

Marily Dumont challenges the received notions of superiority of the English language and calls it the 'Devil's language' (*Ibid.* 391-92). In 'Micmac Hieroglyphics,' Rita Joe points out that the Micmacs had employed the method of preserving their language. They had carved figures on birch barks signifying word, 'beautified with wampum of bead works and quills." These were the Micmac hieroglyphics/ the written word of the Indian/ that the world chooses to deny' (*Ibid.* 114).This script is easier for the First Nations children to grasp.

Accepting the expediency of the English language, Walcott draws his present accommodating Creole language including the French-based and English-based dialects of the Caribbean in his 'The Schooner Flight' covertly bewailing his loss of identity. This loss of identity and shadowy existence of the First Nations in contemporary society is bemoaned by Charlotte Declue in her poem 'Place of Many Swans' (Green 77-78). In the distant past, they had a harmonious existence and the First Nations are able only to bewail that content past, unable to recuperate it in their handicapped existence.

The poems in *Breath Tracks* reflect the First Nations' reverence for the earth and their spiritual connection with nature. The First Nations cultures of America had accorded respect for all beings on the earth. Greg Young-Ing in his poem 'Earth Memory (*Gatherings*, vol. 3) states about the earth:

The oldest Elder
The wisest teacher
The ultimate survivor Creation Warrior. (70)

In the First Nations perception, the community is more important than the individual. Everything is for the enjoyment of the community, not for personal possession. This strongly collectivist cultural value of the First Nations maintains their society as a harmonious one, which is in sharp contrast to the egocentric disposition of the colonizers. In 'Rocks' (*Breath Tracks* 21) the collective feeling of the community is stressed; the ecological imbalance is caused by the unscrupulous devastation of the land by the European occupation. The poet juxtaposes the two cultures to be weighted and valued.

This attitude of First Nations to nature is again reflected In the poem 'First Peoples'

Humbly I take
Only to complete
A Trust that oases hand to hand
Downward
Toward tomorrow
I celebrate creation. (27)

On reaching the Indian lands of rich resources, the Europeans who remain symbols of overexploitation of resources, recklessly destroyed the various species for fun, as theirs was an anthropocentric culture. Many of these species have become extinct. Murray Porter accuses the Europeans in his poem titles '500 years.'

You took us from our homes,
Our language, and our land

> Forget all that we've learned
> Not by choice but by demand. (Young-Ing 281)

He also warns that humans are expected to take only according to his needs, from the earth and excesses will result in the ruin of the earth. The First Nations, who exploited the minimum resources for subsistence, are now being barred from pursuing their traditional means of subsistence.

Nora Devenhauer Sati points out the irony in the white Government's measures to preserve certain species, which they thought were about to be extinct in the poem 'Genocide':

> Picketing the Eskimo
> Whaling Commission
> An over-fed English girl
> Stands with a sign
> 'Let the whales live.' (Green 69)

Armstrong again enlists into service her usual technique of juxtaposition in 'Echo Revelation' (*Breath Tracks* 94) to dislodge the received notions on First Nations' culture and religion. In 'Untitled' (*Breath Tracks* 174), Armstrong stresses the First Nations' values and culture and their relation to the earth. Armstrong's poem 'First People' is a celebration of the pre-contact First Nation world. 'History Lesson' (*Breath Tracks* 28) is a sarcastic record of the gradual taking over of the land by Europeans and the systematic sweeping away of the First Nations. The poet challenges the given history by the Europeans and exposes the hollowness of their boasts. The poem projects the destruction of the ecofriendly culture of the First nations by the so-called civilized whites.

Dan Crank's 'Life Rhythms' celebrates the inseparability of the people and the land:

> in the land is reality
> There is warmth, growth,
> And bountifulness.

And all around, there are the life rhythms.
Like in a living room: plants stretch
to hear the pulse of the music. (Perrault and Vance 138)

Armand Garnet Ruffo points out how the Europeans made the First Nations sign treaties and left them landless and powerless to resist. The poem suggests that the Europeans with their fire-power took away all that had been the sole passion of the First Nations. The poet also hints at the fact that the Europeans are impostors in these lands as they belong to a faraway place (Young-Ing 2 65).

Bren Kolsen bewails the Métis loss of land 'we're the daughters of the Métis. Don't have any land.' She remembers that the white man came and took all the land from their grandparents. She expresses nostalgia at the content past of the Métis that is lost with the arrival of the whites (Perrault and Vance 129). Kateri Damn argues that the Europeans who wield power in First Nations land succeeded in falsifying their history. The history given by the Europeans is full of 'lies' and 'half-forgotten truths' (Young-Ing 2 32).

Nourbese Philip resorts to the potency of her poems to lash out the colonizers' discursive devices to arbitrarily impose labels and identities of the colonized. Armand Garnet Ruffo presents the effects of the white occupation of First Nations lands. All traces of First Nations' life is erased and another culture is imposed there.

Where traditional homelands have been flooded
Clear cut and minded in the name of Progress,
Where one half of the world's population starves
While the other half grows fat in both Body and Mind
Where law means wealth and power and a strong arm
Carrying a big stick, and where justice is just another Word. (41)

In the poem 'Jacob' (Moses and Goldie 129), Maria Campbell points out how the European naming of the First Nations people results in losing trace of their people. In the government records, they indiscreetly attribute European names to First Nations people. Often the persons themselves are unaware of their Europeanized names and thus lose their identity.

Mohawk Writer Pauline Johnson's poem 'The Corn Husker' (Moses and Goldie 31) depicts the predicament of the present-day Indian woman. The Indian woman who now labours in the fields of the Europeans remembers her past. Pauline Johnson challenges the white stance that the Indians are thieves. She portrays how the Whites pursued and slaughtered an Indian chief—Eagle Chief—for thieving the cattle of the white settlers. She asserts that the whites are the thieves. They took all the possessions of the First Nations and dares to impose their morals on the First Nations and judges them with it:

> You have cursed and called him a Cattle
> Thief, though,
> You robbed him first of bread—
> Robbed him and robbed my people. (Moses and Goldie 29)

In the poem 'Letter to Sir John A. Macdonald' (Moses and Goldie 390-91), Marilyn Dumont challenges the settler's government. Administrators like Macdonald who suppressed the First Nations for the convenience of the white settlers. The poet points out that even when the First Nations were facing suppression for centuries, they were able to hold on to what little they had. They are optimistic about the future.

Unable to grasp First Nation language, culture and history, the colonizers imposed their own culture and language on them to retain the First Nations in subjugation. Louise Halfe remembers how she had taken the food prepared in the First Nations way to school. She loved the food, but was ashamed of eating it in the presence of the white kids:

> for school I had your bannock and fried rabbit
> I'd eat it kimoc in the bathroom so the White kids

Wouldn't laugh at me. Ohit was good, so Good.
(Moses and Goldie 370-71)

Bard Fraser satirizes the attitude of the whites toward the First Nations and their subordinate status in the society. Taking the First Nations to be subhuman, the whites attempt to save 'their heathen soul' by Christianizing them. However the whites have no scruples in commercializing the cultural configurations of the First Nations (Young-Ing 2 49).

Chrystos offers resistance to the commodification of the Indian as a parlour showpiece. Images of Indians are sold as parlour showpieces, ignorant of the cultural significance of their regalia. All sorts of attire and feathers of varied colours are exhibited in their images downplaying the cultural significance.

According to the white conceptualization, Indian land and people are to be sold out. The writer says:

I want to bury these Indians dressed like
Cartoons of
Our long dead
I want
To live
Somewhere where nobody is sold. (Fife 78)

This resistance of the commercialization and museumization of the life the Indians is coded by Armstrong in 'Death Murmur' (Fofe 10-11). After callously destroying the Indians and their culture, ironically enough, they are preserving it in museums to be the objects of tax-payers' gaze. The whites are commercializing even from the destruction of the Indian.

Marilyn Dumont thematizes the discrimination accorded to the Indians in the white society in her poem' Memories of a real good brown girl.' The poet implicitly encodes the dynamic of 'us' verses 'them' in this poem. As a child she noticed the difference in nature and appearance of the white girls in her class and herself. She had noticed that her skin is brown whereas the white girls are pale-complexioned. The conjecture that theirs is the ideal complexion inspired the writer's white sister-in-law to bathe and scrub her to make her like the whites.

The deeply ingrained hegemony made a white classmate ask Dumont, seeing her brown hands, 'Are you ever brown!' Dumont confesses that she felt inferior at the question. However later in life, it became comprehensible that there is nothing to be ashamed of in being brown. At school, as she was caught between two worlds, she attempted to imitate the ways of the whites. However on attaining maturity she learned to assert herself by reclaiming her identity (Fife 28-32).

Columpa Bopp bemoans her pain at the denial experienced by the First Nations and expresses her 'raging agony' by 'scream'ing.

> Let me hold the world in my crying hands
> envelope her in my pain
> with the world I shall scream
> the ages of pain away. (Young-Ing 2 46)

Doris Seale encapsulates the predicament of First Nations of contemporary Canadian society and her desire to dismantle the hegemony of the European impostors in the poem 'Will I too Am Through With All that Stuff' (Fife 89-90).

She critiques the European-owned publishing industry's discriminatory practices (Fife 88). Seale painfully observes that even in their own nation, they are deprived of the freedom of expression in their writings. The publishers make it a point to edit the First Nations writings to suit the shared consensus regarding the culture and concept of the First Nations.

Gail Tremblay's fury at the White man's forceful ingression in the Americas is expressed in the poem 'Reveal His Name.' He upholds that a person, who crosses seas and reaches a strange land, destroying the people and culture there, cannot be called an explorer and suggests that his name is 'butcher' (Fife 48).

Undermining European humanism, Walcott rewrites the Christian myth as canonical counter-discourse:

> Adam had an idea.
> He and the Snake would share
> the loss of Eden for a profit,
> So both made the New World.
> And it looked good. (*Collected Poems 1948-1984* 301)

Many of the First Nations poems thematize the nostalgia of the precolonial life and wrath at the destruction of that contented existence. Leonara Hayden Mc Dowell in her poem 'Where Eagles Soar' longs for the past life of the First Nations. She expresses her desire to be in the world of the First Nations that was not stained by the European ingression.

> When my soul is ready to
> Leave this poor shell
> Of shrivelled skin and aching bone,
> My last request to go back home
> Where tall trees grow and eagles fly. (Perrault and Vance 182)

She is tired of accommodating herself in the material culture of the Europeans. African writer Walcott nostalgically reflects on the precolonial existence of the African First Nations:

> There were still shards of an ancient
> Pastoral in those shrines of the island where the
> Cattle drank their pools of shadow from an older sky.
> (*Collected Poems 1948-1984* 383)

Pauline Johnson in 'The Song My Paddle sings' (Mose and Goldie 31) tells the First Nations outdoor life, their attachment to nature. Describing the beauty of nature, the poet suggests the joy of paddling in the river. The Indian way of fishing salmon in the Osoyoos lake and the Okanogan river is nostalgically presented by Harry Robinson in 'Captive Man English Circus' (*Ibid.* 54). They camped near the river and did fishing for some time. He explicates the instance of how a white man badly wounded one among the First Nations who camped there. Even though complaint was lodged, the police did not take any action against the white man. In the settlers' legal systems, the First Nations had no means to know about the charges on them and/ or no means to defend themselves. For any rising against the injustice by the government, inhuman suppressive measures were taken against the First Nations.

Shawn Lynn Danielle Panipekeesick expresses pride at being an Indian. Even though they remain a subjugated class, she is optimistic of a future for the Indians (Perrault and Vance 223). Gayle Weenie in the poem 'Sundance' feels pride at the cultural activities of the First Nations and hints at the mental pleasure it imparts to the participants. She stresses the need for the continuity of ceremonies like the Sundance (*Ibid.* 274). Marie Annharte Baker celebrates the putting of tribal marks on the face by the First Nations. The poem 'Put on My Mask for a Change' is an attempt to revive the First Nations culture (Young-Ing 2 39).

As in fiction and plays, counter-discursive history is promulgated in First Nations poetry to undercut the falsifications propagated by the colonial masters. Frank Conibear is resisting the falsification of First Nations' history in the poem 'Artifacts' (New 9) and asserts that the First Nations know their history and they would continue their oral transmission of it through generations.

The Europeans' destruction of the ecological balance has been the theme of many First Nations poems. The First Nations has maintained the ecological balance for thousands of years, which was destroyed by the white men in the course of their overpowering of the people and the land. In 'The Watchman,' Nancy Cooper is bewailing this fate (Fife 71). Nicole Tanguay again projects this theme in 'Where will the children play.' The once lush evergreen forests are replaced by the concrete forests. What used to be a forest of living creatures turned out to be their slaughter house. The poet bitterly points out that now for the conceptualization of an evergreen forest to your children, you have to show them postcards with the inscription of evergreen forest, another symbol of the Europeans' artificiality. In siphoning off the resources of the earth, the Europeans are not taking into account the seventh generation. The poet asks:

> In seven generations what will be left
> Sky that is made from the deserts
> that used to be rainforests
> houses with no windows to see the
> effects of their forefathers. (Fife 59-60)

Juxtaposing the culture of the colonizers and the resultant predicament of the First Nations, the poet proves that the Europeans' irrational slaughter of nature has turned the First Nations to be destitute and the Europeans are lavishing in plenty. Emma La Roque writes about the sad plight of the First Nations in her 'Eulogy for Priscilla' (Perrault and Vance 141-46). The whites are provokingly indifferent to the First Nations predicament.

As the First Nations maintained an emotional attachment to huge trees, many stories related to trees exist, illustrating this attachment. It is part of their life, as they share their joys and sorrows with these trees. The Metis woman writer Heid Erdrich's pain at the destruction of ecology by the Europeans is reflected in the poem 'The Tree That's Gone' (Fife 106).

The First Nations resent the arrival of Europeans to their lands as it resulted in the causation of their destitution. In the poem 'Suppressed' (Perrault and Vance 238), Elezabeth Robinson accuses that 'the White man causes heartache and destruction' wherever 'they go,' suppressing the people there and spreading diseases like 'small pox.' She remembers how the white man took all their possessions and left the First Nations a hapless community. Louis Erdrich remembers the arrival of early settlers to the continent. In those days the First Nations used to observe the settlers curiously. But the irony is that now the Europeans are commercializing on the First Nations as curiosities (Green 87-

88). In 'The Native Ones' (Fife 120-21), Victoria Lena Manyarrows expresses rancour at the fact that the government still exploit their police force to abuse the First Nations who were the rightful owners of the land. The Europeans desire that First Nations should quit the land leaving it free for the white occupation. Maracle employs the metaphor of a dandelion on Bay street to portray the five-hundred-year-old silence of the First Nations. They are in an enforced silence because nobody was listening to them. Maracle believes that like the dandelions, the First Nations got nothing, 'But still (they) had a grit about the future' (Williamson 167-68).

The Reflections of History
Beatrice Culleton's *In Search of April Raintree* and Maria Campbell's *Halfbreed*

> [The Indian] was seen at his best when hunting. Upon the warpath he was cruel. Tomahawking, scalping and torturing with fiendish ingenuity . . . among his own clansmen he spent his time in gambling, storytelling or taking part in some rude feast. . . . Indian religion was purest superstition. (W.H.P. Clement, *The History of the Dominion of Canada*, 13)

Eminent historians agree that 'history consists of a corpus of ascertained facts' (Carr 9) which reaches the reader after filtering through the mind of the historian. Hence it is manmade; constructive imagination plays a considerable part in it which is taken for granted. Lacking perception of the significance, historians often ignore the cultural bases of available inference and the programs and prejudices of the historian get reflected in the histories they write. Collingwood writes: "History inevitably manoeuvres a strategic presentation of certain views and a suppression of others [making it] a partial and incomplete view of the world, aiming not at knowledge de omni scibili but at knowledge of certain special field, detached from the actuality of what is given in experience, and leaving certain essential elements in that actuality deliberately ignored" (15,138). Edward Said maintains that 'if we agree that all things in history, like history itself are made by men,' it is easy to assume that assigning roles and giving meanings are also done by men (54).

In writing history of First Nations of Canada, European historians pursued discrete agendas, corroborating the documentary accounts left by voyagers and traders that had been shaped and compiled according to the genre and cultural conventions of the Europeans. As Fanon points out 'the settler makes history' with the attitude that if he leaves, 'the country will go back to the middle ages' (*The Wretched of the Earth* 51) As the First Nations depend largely on oral preservation of their history, the mass deaths and epidemics since European contacts obliterated the possibility of the oral recording of their past, as their population dwindled. The Europeans in their official records effected a displacement of First Nations history and substituted it with the imperial history of the colonizers.

Alfred Memmi contends that 'every ideology of combat includes as an integral part of itself a conception of the adversary' (80). In colonial relationships, the characterization and role of the colonized is grounded on this ideology, which impelled the European to have recourse to the distortions of First Nations history to suit their demands; stereotypical dichotomies were imposed on the First Nations which gradually got embedded in the European psyche, creating fear and derision in the First Nations. Said called this ideology Orientalism. Disputes over land rights dissipated the First Nations-European relations. Their closeness to nature led the later writers to associate them with animals, which in turn led to the epithet 'Noble Savage' (Fairchild). Gradually they became static characters distanced from the present and they were treated as the 'other' by the whites. Terry Goldie says in her text *Fear and Temptation* (1993) that this shift in stance occurred in the writings of traders and explorers like Alexander Mackenzie who presume that First Nations possess the vices 'most abhorrent to cultivated and reflecting man' like 'incest' and 'bestiality' (*Voyages* xcvii). In the writings of David Thomson, the European traveller, First Nations are cannibals. He gives the account of Nahathaway man, Wiskahoo, who was 'on the point of eating one of his children to save the others' from hunger (40).

Instead of direct confrontation, treacherous and cruel means were employed to wipe out the occupants of the land. Scalping was one such means. The theoretical perspective on this summed up in *Manichean Aesthetics* (1983) by Abdul R. Jan Mohammed is as follows: 'The dominant model of power and interest relations in all colonial societies is the Manichean opposition between the putative superiority of the European and the supposed inferiority of the Nations.' (65) The following passage from an elementary school textbook in Canada underpins this: 'Their [Indians] ways of living are not at all as they used to, and now instead of going on the warpath and scalping their enemies they are as peaceful as all other Canadians.' (McLauchlan 4)

This is a thorough distortion of history. If the First Nations had been aggressive and warlike, the Europeans could not have occupied the land without any open warfare. Even dignitaries like W.H.P. Clement, a British Columbia supreme Court Judge, were among perpetrators of negative perceptions of the First Nations people. In *History of the Dominion of Canada* (1897), he underscores: "[The Indian] was seen at his best when hunting. Upon the warpath he was cruel. Tomahawking, scalping and torturing with fiendish ingenuity. . . among his own clansmen he spent his time in gambling, storytelling or taking part in some rude feast. . . . Indian religion was purest superstition." (13) This racist prejudice was inherent in European perception and the colonized is always objectified, depersonalized and dehumanized in their representations. 'In those days whenever Indians appeared on television they would go unnamed' as against his white alterity' (Boyce Richardson 11).

The unintelligibility of the First Nations languages to the Europeans brought the assumption that the First Nations had no history or literature, ignoring the vast body of their Orature. To the Europeans, literature is scriptorial. Macaulay in his minutes of 1835 advised the imparting of the knowledge of English language and system of education to the Indians for their intellectual improvement. Ignorant of any of the language of the East, Macaulay dared to comment that 'a single shelf of a good European library was worth the whole Native literature of India and Arabia' (Cartin 80).

With this prejudice they attempted to condition First Nations discourse by imposing Western codes to them. The unsuitability of the First Nations literatures to fit into their genres urged the Europeans to dismiss them as primitive and attempted their acculturation by introducing the Western system of education, engendering the European hegemony and cultural continuity in the New World. The European system of education imparted to First Nations' children implicitly promoted Euro culture and systematically conditioned First Nations children to inferiorisation. First Nations' languages were stifled in these schools and the language, literature and values of the whites inculcated here, made the First Nations children experience dislocation and disinterestedness, resulting in their disablement in the labour market.

Colonialism is far more than political overpowering. Its power structures invade the social, cultural, artistic and religious realms of the colonized and marginalize and subordinate the existing systems and culture of the society to the extent of museumizing it. Since cultural configurations are laden with social meaning in the whites' attempts at the First Nations' acculturation, the basic signifiers of the First Nations' cultural practices were stubbed. In 1884, Sir John Macdonald's government declared the potlatch illegal conjecturing that it only encouraged idleness and waste. However, this law was strictly enforced only by Duncan Campbell Scott when he became the Deputy Superintendent of Indians Affairs. He maintained, 'The potlatches are attended by prolonged idleness and waste of time, by ill-advised and wanton giving away of property and by immorality' (Cole and Chaikin 133). The Blackfoot Sundance and the Cree Thirst dance also were suppressed along with leisure activities like gambling and playing pool, on the pretext that they encouraged the spirit of violence and immorality among the First Nations (Titley 162). Beneath the veneer of such notions lie the hegemonic underpinnings of the Westerners.

Churchmen contributed handsomely towards promoting racism that had been generated by the economic factors of capitalism. Despite the exorbitances and lax behaviour of many of the followers of Christianity, missionaries attempted at deciphering Indian religious practices ensuring the superiority of Christianity. Quoting scriptures, they conjectured that Englishmen 'have a solemn duty to seek out fresh lands to relieve the congestion at home. . . . The Savage occupants of these lands should be cast out' or converted (Wright 93). European theologians justified seizing of the First Nations lands reiterating that Indians were Canaanites to be dispossessed and enslaved by the faithful. Ezra Stiles, president of Yale university theorized that Indians were descendants of the Canaanites who fled from Palestine during Israelite conquests (Haven 4). Drawing from the Darwinian theory, Europeans explained the First Nations incapacity to acculturation. To Arthur Comte de Gobineau, the rise and fall of civilizations is the inevitable consequence of the conquest of an inferior race by a superior one which eventually loses the racial superiority through miscegenation ending up in the decline and fall of that civilization (*The Inequality of Human Races*).

The First Nations shows, presented as entertainments in the 1880s, representing the First Nations cultural configuration were carefully couched to affirm the constructed images of the First Nations, embedded in the Europeans psyche. Prominent among these was the Buffalo Bill show. The enactments of historic events of First Nations life performed in line with the European versions were meant to affirm the European fantasies about the First Nations as a bloodthirsty and aggressive race, still living as savages in teepees, who killed and scalped the European travellers, torturers of women and innocent captives. Further, it celebrated the triumph of European hegemony over the First Nations.

The organizers capitalized on First Nations celebrities like Gabriel Dumont, sitting bull and Black Elk in the early stages of the show. However, perceiving the surreptitious motifs, they quit. Black Elk later commented about his involvement in the show: 'I thought I ought to go, because I might learn some secret of the Wasichu [whites] that would help my people somehow. . . . I know now that this was foolish but I was young and in despair' (Neihardt 219).

The insignia of First Nations cultures is exploited and commodified for advertisements and tourist attraction by the Canadian government. The erections of Totem poles in the prestigious public centres signify this. Further, Indians are accommodated to represent the exotic in a government advertisement, two Indians wearing large brightly coloured masks of raven's head, seated on a beach is given with a headlines: 'Only in God's country could you meet such interesting souls.' Though the advertisement presents Indians as 'Animal People,' in contemporary Canadian society it is clearly factitious. That the Indians in the advertisement are 'spiritual,' 'mysterious Indians' belong to history. They are a part of land, like the animals, in touch with the unseen forces of nature' (qtd. Francis 187-88). Such perverted images were paraded before the public to help justify and legitimize the incarceration of the entire population of First Nations (Adams 38).

The Whites developed theories such as the Great Chain of Being, Social Darwinism and scientific racism (Bynum 13) based on the innate biological characteristics to corroborate their racial subtext. To them, though physically strong, First Nations are mentally weak and therefore they can perform hard labour but should be controlled by the Whites who are more cerebral.

To assert that the First Nations society has many shortcomings, lives of First Nations women were presented as one of drudgery. In missionary version, women had to perform hard labour in the domestic and social sphere which went unrecognized. No humanistic consideration is allowed to them. They were at the mercy of their father/ husband who treat them as mere commodities. When they become old and weak, they were cast out and a new one is taken. John Mc Dougal refers to the 'bartering and slaying' of women in his Book Missionary outlook (53). Eherton Ryerson Young, another missionary, wrote that 'in paganism she [First Nation woman] has not the life of a dog. She is kicked and cuffed and maltreated continually' (148). They claimed that with the coming of Christianity and civilization, the condition of First Nations women has improved considerably.

The European failed to appreciate the social, political and economic applications of First Nations' marriages. The system of marriage varied with different First Nations communities. The presentation of gifts by both parties conjecture that First Nations marriages are a process of bartering. Jane Fishburne Collier in her *Marriage and Inequality in Classless Societies* (1988) states that wives could not be bought for money in Canadian First Nations societies. Presenting gifts to the bride's party is an obligation of the bridegroom. Discussions would be held by both parties regarding mutual obligations, not about price. Initiation of marriage varied with the different tribes. Arranging marriages is the duty of elders (82).

Though First Nations cultures were projected as patriarchal, they were geocentric. The European construction of victim image to First Nations women assigned the role of rescuer to the Europeans' vindication of their presence in the First Nations lands. Projecting the evil social practices imposed on women in the First Nations societies and contrasting it with the assumed superiority of European women, they instilled consciousness of inferiority of First Nations cultures and legitimized the European hegemony.

Two archaeological sites unearthed in the Yukon and Alberta region in the recent past had been identified as belonging to the First Nations of Canada dated previously as 17000 years and 30000 to 60000 years respectively has been re-dated as 1300 and

4000 years old respectively. Despite this re-dating, these finds bulwark the arguments that the First Nations of Canada have no history (McMillan). The remnants of structures unearthed in the Arizona, Colorado, New Mexico and Utah regions suggest that the First Nations of Canada had huge cities consisting of large edifices having four and five storeys including irrigation facilities. Still their architecture was ecofriendly (Friesen).

The First Nations had a primordial relationship with land and maintained the ecological balance as against the Europeans' rash siphoning off of resources. An instance of this is recorded in First Nations history. When a White farmer attempted to cut off a tree, a First Nations man objected to it saying: 'If you raise a calf or cabbage you may call it your own, but you can have no claim on that tree . . . that tree was planted by the great spirit for the Micmac before you and your fathers escaped from your murky shells and crossed the great waters' (Whitehead 228).

As against the European construction, the First Nations were a very hospitable people. They had the habit of sharing their acquisitions with the community. Eminent South African sociologist Chbani Maganyi's view of the Black people is applicable to the First Nations people of Canada. Maganyi opines: 'in social relationships the white approach is characterized by the primacy of the individual, the Black approach is characterized by that of the community' (qtd. Pandurang 106). When the settler woman Annie Greer gave birth to her first child in a log cabin west of Manitoba, Caroline the First Nations medicine woman assisted her and it is said that Caroline had further assisted the settler family by providing them with cow to get a start in the new environment without taking any reward (Preston 102-3).

The European travellers and writers polarizing the otherness of the First Nations of the Americans ignored such noble aspects of the First Nations and interiorized their religion and culture exploiting their economic failure. The tension between the rhetorically embellished accounts of travellers and actuality had been ideologically kept in check by the collective European imagination, recapitulating poetic geography drawing from the texts of the antique and far off. The suppressive policies on the First Nations were legitimized by the polarity of the images of the white and the First Nations; the First Nations alterity served to justify their deplorable living conditions and poverty. Marina Heung observes: 'Literally colonization operates by taking over land and bodies. On a symbolic level, it works on bodies because physical anatomies become the canvas on which cultural meanings are projected' (82).

The colonizers wanted to rid the Indians of the land so that it would remain free for European occupation. They applied the technique of setting one Indian tribe against the other. Defeating the tribes who were skilled in guerilla warfare was not so simple. They adopted the policy of extermination of the First Nations through applications of biological weapons like poisoning water sources used by the First Nations, issuing contaminated blankets to the First Nations by which they contacted epidemics etc. Masses of people perished under such deceitful acts. An instance of serving poisoned food to the Micmacs by the British after inviting them to a gathering in 1712 is recorded (Reid 75-76). The white men were barbarians and perpetrators of crime. Pierre Maillard writes that among the earliest victims of Rangers were five Micmacs women and their three children. They were all massacred and the two pregnant women among them had 'their bellies ripped open' (Whitehead 102). The image of Indians as savages embedded in the European consciousness served to vindicate the physical and cultural genocide of the First Nations.

Colonial government's prohibition of interracial marriages was intended to avoid the European inheritance of the progeny. Instead of solving the social and economic problems faced by the First Nations, the colonial government blamed them for their conditions of squalor to deflect criticism of their own shortcoming. The treaties signed by First Nations rendered their hoarding in reserves engendering the setting aside of lands for the settlers.

In the pre-colonial days, the Indians had finally tuned political institutions of governance as waves of settlers penetrated into the Americas First Nations populations were crumbled by the successive onslaught of mass deaths and epidemics. The leaders were faced with the challenge of preempting the extinction of their community on earth and holding on to their sovereignty. The technologically powerful Europeans undermined the Indian culture and practices. Knowing that the settlers' government was determined to take away all their lands, the First Nations had no options but to accept their unequal terms and conditions.

The First Nations offered resistance under the leadership of chief Mistahimaskwa [Big Bear] the great Cree Leader in the 1870s which culminated in the rebellion of 1885 under Louis Riel. But the settlers' government succeeded in splitting the first Nations solidarity and crashing the Rebellion and executing the leaders.

Historians fall back on documenting 'evidence' given out by the White traders and settlers that were largely written to justify the motifs of the whites. In Charles G.D. Roberts's Canadian history, First Nations existence prior to European contact is ahistoric. It only serves to promulgate the negative fictitious image. The Canadian government drew insight from this misleading information for the government of the First Nations. A series of suppressive measures were initiated on the First Nations after the Riel Rebellion and the Red River Rebellion which were the resistance moves on the part of First Nations against White domination. First Nations attempt for legal action against injustice was stifled by making lawyers representing Indians against crown illegal.

The incident at Duck Lake during the Riel Rebellion had been exploited by the Europeans in adding to the negative image of the First Nations. During the period of turbulence, some white men had been shot dead by the First Nations and they sieged a store controlled by the Indian Agency. The actual reason for provocation had been covered up and the 'facts' given out by the white-controlled media were underpinning the tales of horror and savagery of the First nations. The First Nations rounded up some white settlers and missionaries who had been secretly serving as spies of the North West mounted police who had on many occasions ill-treated the First Nations, especially women. The Indians kept the captives at a Cree camp at Frog Creek and the dissidents were shot dead. Dilaney and Gowanlock were two white men thus killed. Their wives were taken as captives (Stanely 164-65).

Confusion still exists about the number of deaths and the perpetrators of the crime. Historian Hugh Demsey writes: 'If everyone is to be believed, nine victims at Frog Lake must have been buried more often than a dog's favourite bone' (214-15). According to First Nations writer Joe Dion, Big Bear had made arrangements for the safety of two women captives (91-92).

With the intention of sullying the image of the Indians, the white eroded the original statements made by the two widows about the incident and the First nations are represented as stereotypical villains in the written accounts of captivity published in the name of the two women (*Life and Adventures* 83-91).The two women captives who had remained with the Crees during the period of trouble followed the Indians when they tried to avoid capture by troops, later left the captors with their permission. As the church authorities were in collusion with the federal government, many priests worked as informants to the government against the Métis interests. The Métis trusted their priests and expressed their views unsuspecting the trustworthiness of their priests.

After the fall of Batoche and Riel's surrender, the troops pursued Big Bear and the captives. Big Bear surrendered himself at Hunsdon's Bay Company of his own accord. None of the hostages had been rescued by the troops. They had returned on their own (Morton 127-44).

Though the 1885 Rebellion was the First Nations fight for freedom from a colonial government, it was interpreted as a rising against the rightful government and the participants were labelled as 'traitors' and denied justice (Adams 101). Europeans' firmly entrenched racial prejudices and First Nations stereotyping is evident in the report of the 1885 Battle of Duck Lake. "A band of police on a lawful errand and been obstructed by armed rebels, loyal Canadian citizens had been killed and wounded by halfbreeds and Indians—these could be interpreted only as the acts of a savage and lawless mob threatening the west with murder and pillage." (Department of Indian Affairs and Northern Development 7)

Howard Adams mentions that he felt the need to assess the primary sources on the 1885 Rebellion, finding the contradictions in history books, especially when one French Canadian writer points out that 'the history books on the Métis were misleading' (101).

In spite of his American citizenship Louis Riel, the leader of the 1885 Rebellion, was charged with treason. Though the trial was held as per the rules of the judiciary, 'It seems to have unfolded according to intrigues and conspiracies, collaborations and collusions among the power politicians and capitalists within their vested interests.' Three men were there to give evidence to all the Métis prisoners, even when the actual participants of the trial were available in the prison to testify. The defence lawyers who were whites did not seriously cross-examine the witnesses. They were not defending Riel (Adams 109, 113-14).

Riel had incurred the displeasure of the church authorities by refusing to oblige to their tyranny. Though deeply religious, when the priests refused to serve the Métis in their religious activities, Riel advised them against the Church tyranny. He felt that the church was part of the colonial power stratifications. But his moves against the church were interpreted as blasphemy and priests were ready to testify against him.

Adams points out some of the discrepancies found in the documents 'that were reported to have been found in the rebels' council room in Batoche on 12th May 1885, which were thought to be belonging to Riel (10). The documents show that the First Nations fighters were well-organized after the European military fashion and they had strict time schedule for their routine. Adams asserts that there is every reason to believe that these documents of the insurgents' could be false or contrived as 'many of the statements and the topics in the documents are conspicuously incongruous with the reality of the halfbreed situations.' The Métis do not meet in the formal style and they could not have 'motions' by 'movers' and 'secondary,' and they do not address each other as 'Mister' before their first name. Since they were involved in a guerrilla war, they could not be thought of foolish enough to keep such documents of their activities. Further, the words and expressions used in the documents are also not common among the Métis (Adams 101-3).

Thought Louis Riel had been the hero of the Métis, the leader of their resistance struggle against the colonizers, he had not been considered a dominant figure by the whites. Sir Joseph Pope in his *Days of Sir John Macdonald* (1915) writes about Riel that he was 'a wretched malefactor' actuated by personal ambitions (qtd. Francis and Smith 104-6).

Riel and his rebellion is ahistoric to the writers of *Chronicles of Canada* (1914-16) series published during World War I, suggesting the invisibility of the First Nations in the Canadian diasporas. The French Catholic writers gave a different stature to Riel. To them, he was a martyr who fought against 'English vindictiveness' and 'protestant bigotry' (*Ibid.* 104-8).

European-controlled media competed in portraying First Nations women as the instigators of violence, exploiting the Duck Lake incidents. The women were portrayed as brutal and blood thirsty (*Free Press* 20 May 1885). Reports that 'stony squaws' had horribly mutilated the body of some of the Ottawa sharpshooters who had been killed at the battle of Catnife Hill 'created the utmost indignation in camp and threats loud and deep are uttered on all sides [sic] against the Indians' (*Free Press* 2 June 1885). Baseless rumours that the 'squaws' had won from Riel the privilege to slaughter the women of the settler community if their town comes under siege served to inflame hatred and resentment among the terrified settler community (Abrams 79).

Out of such misconceptions of First Nations brutality evolves the theme of a ballad by the white Dr. T.A. Patrick. But the squaws were the worst of these-demons accurst, 'With the spirit of war and of woe/ For they would have shot those two men on the spot/ And they aimed with the arrow and bow. (qtd. Hawkes 226) Whereas the press gave wide coverage to the sufferings of the white community during the rebellion, the deaths and sufferings of First Nations people received little coverage or sympathy.

The First Nations temperament is for hunting and trapping. Forced to abandon their ways of subsistence, the Indians desperately attempted to pursue an agricultural economy though it was incompatible with their culture and temperament which again was stifled by the governmental regulations. The Department of Indian Affairs conspicuously pursued a restrictive policy to thwart the First Nations attempts to create an agricultural economy. Application of European technology was forbidden to First Nations farmers. They neither had the right to sell their goods outside the Reserves nor had the freedom to decide the price of their goods. By keeping away Indian farmers from the markets, the Whites propagated that the measure is to teach the lazy Indians to be self-dependent and attributed the First Nations' incapacity to pursue an agricultural economy characteristic of their racial typology.

Those who urged to monitor the movement of the First Nations desired that the First Nations products should not be marketed in the settlements, which would facilitate less competition in the markets allowing white farmers to control the markets economy. The introduction of the pass system since the turbulent period of 1885 was to keep away the First Nations from joining the rebels. Moving out of the Reserve necessitated the possession of a pass issued by the Indian Agent or Farm Inspector. The white settlers felt that the pass system was too lenient and the First Nations should be strictly confined to their Reserves.

Consequent to all these stipulative measures, Reserve Lands remained centres of ill-health and poverty. The Department of Indian Affairs pre-empted any criticism, blaming the inherent indolence of the First Nations. Colonization gave definite financial gain to the colonizers. When the federal government spent two billions on First Nations over a century, it gained around sixty billion dollars from the colonies. The federal government spent $530 per Treaty Indian per year whereas it spent $740 per non-Native (Frideres et al 8). To deal the famine after the First World War, the government gave orders to take on lease the uncultivated Indian lands without the permission of the Indians and cultivate these under the supervision of government agent. The measure effected in the Indian's losing control of their land and the government gained about seventy-five million acres of Reserve lands. As Fanon observes: '[the First Nations] represent not only the absence of values but also the negation of values . . . they are the depository of maleficent power and the unconscious and irretrievable instrument of blind forces.' (qtd. Hayes 16)

The British Columbia newspaper, *The Native Voice*, compares the condition of the First Nations 'to the poor man in the Gospel who lived of the crumbs that fell from the rich man's table. . . . This is particularly galling to us, as the table and what is on it was at one time exclusively our own, and we intend to, and do demand our rightful position on terms of equality with our fellow Canadians' (qtd. Richardson 132)

Stories of savagery and licentiousness of First Nations people were spread to promote scheme of strict confinement of Indians to the Reserves. These stories helped the acceleration of racist consensus among white populations. While sex and violence are exploited as manifestations of the decadence of the First Nations society, alcohol is presented as another significant aspect of First Nations nature. The violence committed by the First Nations by the consumption of alcohol points to the violence done by the whites to the First Nations. With the First Nations, violence becomes a symbol of the loss of their traditional values. Whereas before the Riel Rebellion, First Nations women were represented as drudges who enjoyed no freedom, the image turned out into one of dominating and dangerous. They were represented as the instigators of violence. In fact, violence was part of the Whites' imperialistic agenda. The Charter of King Chrles I of England to the colonial government in Canada authorizes this violence on the First Nations people: 'collect troops and wage on the barbarians, and to pursue them even beyond the limits of their province and if God shall grant it, to vanquish and captivate them: and the captives put to death' (Friederes et al 19).

Peter Farb points out that in the early stages, white settlers 'offered to pay bounties on dead Indians' and the idea of scalping was originated by Governor Kieft of New Netherland (124). The colonial government availed the assistance of Mohawks to track down the Micmacs who were skilled in guerilla warfare. Thus forming companies of Boston Rangers, they hunted down the Micmacs and scalps of the murdered Indians were taken, for which they were rewarded handsomely. Offering bounties on the scalp of Indian were in effect from the 1750s. In 1754, a crew of shipwrecked whitemen was saved by the Indians at Halifax. They in turn killed the Indians for scalps and claimed premium from the authorities (Reid 76). Considering the portability, scalp is 'accepted as proof that an Indian has been killed.' By paying 'liberally' for scalps, the Europeans 'virtually cleared southern New York and New Jersey' for the settlers (Farb 124). However the whites doled out that because of the laziness and lack of 'foresight' of the Micmacs, they fail to 'enjoy' 'the benefits of civilization—arts, science and laws' (qtd. Upion 139).

Jenny Sharpe argues that circulation of stories of violence by the colonized and attempts at the honour of white women were strategies of covering up the failures of imperial governmental machinery. Fabricated stories of tortures underwent by White captives were given out to justify horrifying repressive measures taken against colonial risings. Sharpe points out at an incident during Indian Sepoy mutiny of 1857. The colonial government succeeded in projecting the image of the mutineers as brutal savages. When the British army approached to confront the mutineers at Lucknow who held British civilians as hostages, the hostages were executed. Though it was an exceptional action, the colonizers projected it to substantiate their tales of horrors of the East (Sharpe 61-64).

Natasha Kzanzek points out that the exhibits in the Royal Ontario Museum reveal a lot about the European ego and their atrocities on the First Nations as well as the horrors of destruction. There is an illustration of a British soldier on horseback driving his sword through a shield into the chest of an African who is on foot. It has the caption 'Lord Beresford's encounter with a Zulu.' Here, to the Europeans, encounter means killing. In another illustration, four Africans who are carrying the belongings of a white man and woman on horseback are pictured like animals. In another depiction, standing above several African women, a white woman makes them scrub her cloths. The caption for the picture is: 'Taken in Nigeria about 1910, this photograph shows missionary Mrs. Thomas Titcombe giving African women a lesson on how to wash clothes.' These depictions appear under the plaque heading 'civilization commences and Christianity.' Thus the Christian missionaries in the name of civilizing the First Nations were exploiting and enslaving them (Itwaru and Kzanzek 82-86).

The Canadian government's authoritarian predispositions

and ethnic prejudices were blatant in the handling of the Oka Revolt. When a golf course was planned to be constructed on the sacred grounds of the First Nations, they put up resistance. The authorities succeeded in creating the impression that the First Nations are irresponsible trouble-makers impeding the progress. The whites' contempt of the Indians is discernible in the writings of Francis Parkman that Indians were 'like badly disciplined children,' 'lying, treacherous deceitful capricious, jealous, refractory and predisposed to violence.' He employs metaphors like 'dusky mistresses,' 'shrivelled hags' and 'mongrel offspring' to describe Indian women and children. The Indian names were 'barbaric appellatives' when compared to the Christian names of the Europeans. He describes Chief Donnacona as a 'greasy potentate' (31-53).

Even language is exploited as a tool in degrading the Indian people aiming at their cultural genocide and the potential of translation is explored to propagate the pejorative perceptions about the First Nations and justify the 'asymmetrical relations of power that operate under colonialism' (Niranjana 2). In Richard Burton's translation of *The Arabian Nights* (1885-88), the Western prejudices and constructs of Eastern tales is discernible. Indian names are mocked by giving incorrect and anglicized versions. When English version of First Nations names are given out for the convenience of the white, no white name is translated for the intelligibility of the First nations.

In the official government pronouncement of treaty negotiations, Indian are infantilized as wards of the Queen. Governor Morris addresses the Indians in this fashion for the signing of Treaty Six 'Indian children of the Queen. . . . I am glad to learn that they [Crees] are looking forward to having their children civilized' (qtd. Adams 40). Referring to the Indians by numbers instead of names was part of the dehumanization and depersonalization tactics. Until recently the Indian Agent had the right to interfere in the personal affairs of the Indians to the extent that he could even open their personal mail.

With the extinction of the buffalos and the prairies where they roamed, the First Nations lost their food supply and their way of life. Gradually they were confined to Reserves by the federal government which meant the loss of political and economic freedom engendering the sole dependence on the humiliating experience of government welfare for subsistence. Recalcitrant were forced to oblige. In the Qu'Appelle region, Chief Yellow Calf and some others of his tribe refused to be confined to Reserves. Though they could withstand the police force for two months, subsequent reinforcement of troops from Regina herded them into Reserves, crushing their resistance.

The colonialist imposition of capitalism left the First Nations jobless. They would be given only menial unskilled jobs, which the whites won't take. Hard tasks like firefighting were compulsory for First Nations people. Indians could not establish a family grounded on their occupational status and income as they were given only causal and seasonal jobs depending on the labour market capacities and capabilities. Though joblessness was one cause of Indians' poverty, the authorities attributed it to laziness.

Instead of providing any means of subsistence to the First Nations or listening to their supplication, the federal government spent lavishly on maintaining Mounted Police to suppress their resistance against denial of rights. A North Battleford priest wrote about the condition of Indians in 1883: 'the cakes made with some bad flour did not satisfy the appetite of the Indians. I saw the gaunt children, dying of hunger come to my place. Although it was 30 to 40 below Zero, their bodies were scarcely covered with torn rags' (*Advertiser* 31 March 1884).

Europeans employed their advanced science and technology to intimidate the First Nations people. The Federal Government and Indian Agents were keen on exacerbating tribal rivalries, encouraging sectarian differences. The Indians were divided into small bands and the Indian agents took it as their duty to sow dissention among the bands, spreading rumours of intolerance and animosity of the neighbouring bands, building up suspicion of their own people in the First Nations minds, which in turn kept them divided. Cashing in on the strife among the tribes and the comparative peace among the colonizers, the appearance of civilization and superiority was gained by the Europeans.

Allegations of sexual advances by Europeans on First Nations women often ended up in the rebounding of the allegation on First Nations women. Most often, First Nation women were victimized. In 1880, defending the North West Mounted Police men, the Toronto *Globe* wrote that First Nations women were lascivious and were 'notorious the world over' for their immorality. They argued, 'no men in the world are so good as to teach them [First Nations Women] better or to try to reform them in this respect' (4 June 1880). The *Toronto Daily Mail* even wrote that Aboriginal men were selling their women and children to the white men since the initial stage of fur trade. They claimed that the police had done a lot to terminate this practice (2 Feb. 1886). In fact, in the initial stage of settlement, whites especially the Royal Canadians Mounted Police men, forcefully took First Nations girls for wives and in some cases after giving grocery to the starving families of the girls and propagated that the First Nations females are whores (Turner 10).

The Department of Indian Affairs and Northern Development remained bigoted in their dealings with the First Nations. Many government employees related to First Nations Reserves abused their positions for exploiting the First Nations. Cases of farm instructor demanding sexual favours from young girls were common. If the demand was turned down, measures like cutting ration and inflicting all sorts of restrictions on the family, were employed by the officials. There was the instance of Chief Crowford of the Blackfoot complaining to the authorities that the farm instructor on their Reserve demanded sexual favours from young girls in return for rations. On investigation, it was found that the culprits go scot-free since their own men conducted the enquiry. In accusations of immorality against the North West Mounted Police, the editor of the *Macleod Gazette*, an ex-North West Mounted Policeman, wrote: 'nothing is said about the fact that many of these women were prostitutes before they went to live with the white men, and that in the majority of cases the Nurtures [sic] for this so-called immorality come from the women or Indians themselves.' (16 March 1886).

According to him, the white men were only 'taking advantage of an Indian offer' (23 March 1886). In 1914, the Superintendent General of Health was authorized to ensure the health conditions of the First Nations as in the European concept, First Nations homes were unfit and unhygienic for human habitation. Thus the superintendent became an unquestioned authority over First Nations homes. Further, the wills made by the Indians were to be approved by the Superintendent General. He had complete authority to accept or reject these wills. Repressive measures could be taken on recalcitrant. Many of the government employees killed at Frog Lake and Battleford during the turbulent period were intensely hated by the First Nations communities as they were callous and exploited the First Nations, especially women. The farm instructor James Payne who was killed at Frog Lake during the period was accused for the death of a First Nations girl. Finding this girl visiting his young First Nations wife, the furious man beat her and threw her out of his house. The girl died soon after and her father blamed Payne for her death. Payne was shot at by this man, during the turbulence of Frog lake in 1885 (Paget 13-15).

The case of Maria Thomas is another instance of racism of the whites. Maria Thomas, a sixteen-year-old Metis girl, was serving in the homestead of Reverent Griffith Owen Corbett. Corbett the master of the house was found guilty of seducing the girl and was sentenced to six months' imprisonment. Focusing on this incident, the newspapers competed to justify the action of the white man and blame the victim, the teenager.

Erica Smith writes how the local newspapers gave the coverage of its trial. They projected Abigail Smith, the wife of the accused, for acquitting the accused. Ladies like Abigail Smith were the embodiment of womanly virtue 'sterling character, noble sentiments, refined emotion, genteel deportment and most important sexual purity' whereas First Nations women like Maria Thomas were lecherous 'articulated inappropriate sexual knowledge and gadded about in public destroying the domestic happiness of respectable families and reputations of respectable neighbourhood' (367-70). Thus as Terry Goldie puts it, the First Nations become 'a semiotic pawn on a chessboard under the control of the white sign maker' (10).

In Beatrice Culleton's *In Search of April Raintree*, April had a heritage of mixed nationalities. Her father was "a little bit of this and a little bit of that and a whole lot of Indian." April's mother was part Irish and part Ojibway. April inherited her mother's pale skin, while Cheryl inherited her father's darker skin. when April and Cheryl went to play in the park, the white kids and the native children were calling each other names. April's mom got fatter and fatter one year. She went to the hospital and came home with a new baby, named Anna. 'Anna's sick,' the woman answered. 'She's gone to the hospital. Don't worry; we'll take you for a ride to a nice clean place. You and Cheryl, okay' (17).

Anna was sick, however, and eventually the child and family services people came to pick up April and Cheryl since they did not feel that it was fit for them to live with their parents. April and Cheryl were taken to live with nuns until a foster home was found. Cheryl and April got separated and placed in different foster homes. Cheryl went to live with the MacAdams family and April went to live with the Dions. 'Mrs. Dions, my new foster mother, spoke up. For some reason, she reminded me of my mother.' (22) 'What's your new home like? Mrs. Semple told me you live with the MacAdams. Are they nice?' (26)

Both families were very kind to the girls and they progressed rapidly. At the end of the chapter, Mrs. Dion gets sick and April must be moved to a new foster home. April now gets placed with the DeRosiers. The mother and her children, Maggie and Ricky, are very mean to April. They make her do all the house work and refer to her as a "halfbreed":

> The school bus comes at eight. You will get up at six, go to the hen house, and bring back the eggs. While I prepare breakfast, you will wash the eggs. After breakfast, you will do the dishes. After school, you'll have more chores to do, and then you will help me prepare supper. After you do the supper dishes, you will go to your room and stay there. You'll also keep yourself and your room clean. I know you half-breeds; you love to wallow in filth. (38)

This makes April feel resentful to her heritage and she begins to look down on the fact that she is Métis. Cheryl, on the other hand, takes interest in Métis history and looks up to her heritage with a sense of pride. April discovers that her parents weren't ever really sick and that they were actually just alcoholics, she doesn't tell this to Cheryl though. Cheryl comes to live with April at the DeRosiers. She stands up to the DeRosiers more than April ever did; as a result, April also becomes more aggressive. The De Rosier children didn't do as well as April and Cheryl in school. That was one of the only things that April and Cheryl could hold over the DeRosiers. Maggie and Ricky tried to play a trick on Cheryl one day. They told her that the dog named Rebel was hurt. Cheryl went running into the field where the bull was in order to help Rebel. Unfortunately, the bull began chasing Cheryl and she was very badly wounded. Mr. De Rosier saw the whole incident and, for the first time, stood up for April and Cheryl. Cheryl also had some trouble in school. She argued in history class that the book was not correctly portraying the native people.

> If this is history, how come so many Indian tribes were wiped out? How come they haven't got their land anymore? How come their food supplies were wiped out? Lies! Lies! Lies! Your history books don't say how the white people destroyed the Indian way of life. That's all you white people can do is teach a bunch of lies to cover your own tracks! (57)

She got a strapping from the principal and her hair cut off by Mrs. De Rosier. One day social workers came for a visit. April thought that they were coming to take Cheryl away. April and Cheryl decided to run away. They were caught and Mrs. Semple gave them a speech on how the things they were doing now, such as lying, running away and feeling sorry for themselves, was going to lead pregnancy and prostitution one day. She also talked about the 'nativegirl' syndrome: 'and you girls are headed in that direction. It starts out with the fighting, the running away, the lies. Next come the accusations that everyone in the world is against you. There are the sullen, uncooperative silences, the feeling sorry for yourselves. And when you go on your own, you get pregnant right away, or you can't find or keep jobs. So you'll start with alcohol and drugs, from there, you get into shoplifting and prostitution, and in and out of jails. You'll live with men who abuse you. And on it goes. You'll end up like your parents, living off society. In both your cases, it would be a pity because Miss Turner knew you both when you were little. And you both were remarkable youngsters. Now, you're going the same route as many other native girls. If you don't smarten up, you'll end up in the same place they do. Skid row!' (66)

Maggie and Ricky start rumours about April. April loses all her friends and the guidance counsellor even confronts her about these things. Cheryl continues to be interested in her heritage and sends April letters containing history papers she has written. April was forced to wear ugly clothing to school. Mrs. De Rosier also didn't give her the mail that Cheryl was sending. Jennifer, a former friend of April, helped her in both these areas. April finally finds a way to get rid of the DeRosiers.

> 'Why don't you write about your life with the DeRosiers?' Jennifer asked with a grin. I thought it was a great idea. But then I said, 'It has to be a Christmas story, and they have a way of destroying Christmas for me.'
>
> For a week I pondered over how I could work my life at the DeRosiers into a Christmas story. Finally, the idea came to me, and I worked on my story at lunchtimes. The title was 'What I Want for Christmas,' and I ended the story with the sentence, 'What I want for Christmas is for somebody to listen to me and to believe in me.' (82)

She writes a Christmas story for a contest and incorporates parts of her life at the DeRosiers. As a result, her teachers believe her and at spring break, she is transferred to St. Bernadette's Academy to finish school.

Cheryl is at this point living with a foster family called the Steindalls. April went there over holidays while she was attending St. Bernadette's Academy. While April was attending St. Bernadette's Academy, she told one really big lie. She was still looking down on her heritage and told all her friends there that her parents had died in a plane crash and that they were no longer living. "I told my friends that my parents died in a plane crash. I didn't plan on that lie. It just came out on the spur of the moment, when I was being asked about my family. They were so sympathetic towards me that I knew I would never be able to take those words back. I credited my ability to make friends easily to the fact that none of them knew I was part Indian." (89)

One summer, April opted to go get a job in Winnipeg instead of spending time with Cheryl. She got introduced to the night life and some other elements of that type of living. Cheryl was slightly offended and disappointed that April didn't come to see her. Both April and Cheryl are free from being foster children. April tried to look for her parents in the slums but soon decided that it was better not to search for them. April had now become a secretary and worked for Mr. Lord. Cheryl decides to become a social worker, so she attends the University of Winnipeg. Garth Tyndall was Cheryl's white boyfriend from university. He seemed to like Cheryl but was embarrassed to be seen with her; Cheryl eventually dumped him. Jerry McAllister was a university professor and became April's boyfriend. He tried to coax April into being physical with him. One day April phoned his house and discovered that he was actually a married man. Roger Maddison was a lawyer at the firm where April worked. He and April had a bit of a rivalry going and they never said anything nice to each other. Bob Radcliffe was April's first husband. He came to Winnipeg on business and met April at the law firm where she worked. He was a gentleman and also very wealthy. He swept April off her feet and they got married. "The events of the next several weeks are blurring in my memory. Bob proposed. He asked me, April Raintree, to be his wife. He wanted to get married in a small civil ceremony in Winnipeg. My dreams were coming true, and I ecstatically floated on cloud nine. Everything happened so quickly" (109).

April moves to Toronto with her new husband, Bob Radcliffe. She is shocked when she sees their new home and realizes just how wealthy Bob really is. Bob's mother lives with them and is very domineering. Cheryl comes to visit April in her new home. She and April don't get along so well and it becomes apparent how far they have drifted apart. April has attained her goal of becoming wealthy and is accepted into white society. Cheryl thinks April is a fake and realizes just how much April looks down on the native heritage that she looks up to. Cheryl wants to search for their parents so April gives her the addresses she has, but doesn't mention to Cheryl that she knows her parents were drunkards. 'Cheryl and I looked at each other for a few silent seconds and our tempers were forgotten. Then she said in a quite accusing voice. 'You went to look for Mom and Dad? How come you never told me, April?' I sighed and wondered which way to go. 'There was nothing to tell. I never found them. I came to a dead end. And later, when I thought it over, I figured it was probably just as well. Finding them would most likely have opened old wounds for them and for us' (118).

Cheryl has left Toronto and April is all alone. She is envious of Cheryl because Cheryl has a point to living. April begins to see all of her rich, high society friends as a bunch of hypocrites. April also discovers that her husband, Bob, is having an affair with Heather Langdon. She is upset and asks him for a divorce and moves into an apartment in Toronto. Letters from Cheryl begin to come less and less frequently. April gets a phone call from the Health Services Centre in Winnipeg saying that Cheryl is in hospital. April flies back to Winnipeg to be with Cheryl. Cheryl has been under the influence of alcohol and is suffering from hypothermia. April discovers that Cheryl has quit university and has been living with a man named Mark De Soto for the last two years. Cheryl asks April to go and pick up things from Mark's place because she doesn't want to live there anymore. April goes to Mark's place on Elgin Avenue. When she tries to go into the house, some men grab her. They take her out to a remote area and rape her. April is thrown out of the back of the truck and she goes to get help at a nearby farmhouse. They call the police and she is taken to the hospital to get checked. She is emotionally, physically and mentally affected by the incident. Deep down, she blames Cheryl. April goes back to Toronto for her divorce hearing and gets money from Bob. She and Cheryl decide to buy a house and a car and live in Winnipeg. April meets Roger Maddison again. This time they become friends and go out for dinner. Roger lets April talk about what has been going on in her life and they become good friends.

> Friday evening started out with both Roger and I trying to make polite conversation. I guess he was as uncomfortable as I was. After the meal, I was sipping coffee when I asked him, 'Roger, how come you were so nasty to me when I worked there?'

> 'I liked you,' he smiled.
>
> 'Well, that was no way to treat someone you liked.'
>
> 'Well, I got your attention, didn't I? Until that man came along.'
>
> 'I did like you, you know,' I said. 'I hated you, too. I hated liking you. Of course, if I had known you liked me, then maybe things would have been different.' (155)

April and Cheryl move into their new home. Roger and April become even better friends although April resists romantic advances. April is still noticing that Cheryl is still having some trouble with alcohol. She and Cheryl attend a Powwow which seems to rekindle Cheryl's interest in native rights. The preliminary hearings for April's rape trial are also underway. One of the men involved had already been arrested. Cheryl takes April to the Friendship Centre. They meet some of Cheryl's friends and April gets to meet one of the elders, White Thunderbird Woman.

April's rape trial continues. One of the men testifies that Cheryl Raintree is a well-known prostitute. April is shocked. At the end, one of April's rapists is found guilty. April feels sorry for herself and Roger tells her that she should just let herself be healed and stop worrying about it. Cheryl becomes extremely distant and is rarely seen by April except when she is drunk. She had found their father and discovered the truth about him. She also discovered that their mother had committed suicide by jumping off the Louise Bridge.

Cheryl leaves and never comes back. Roger and April frantically look for Cheryl. They have no idea where she went and they look for several weeks for her. One night, Nancy, Cheryl's friend, phoned April and told her that Cheryl had been living with her. Cheryl had left suddenly and Nancy thought she was going to do something bad. April phoned the police. It then occurred to her that Cheryl might try to jump off the Louise Bridge, just like their mother did. When they arrived at the Bridge, people standing around said that a woman had jumped off about five minutes earlier.

They discovered that Cheryl had killed herself. Roger helped make all the funeral arrangements. April goes through Cheryl's journals and discovers in more depth what Cheryl had been going through. She discovered that Cheryl actually had a son, Henri Liberty, and that he was living with Nancy right now. For the first time, April didn't look down on her native heritage. It took Cheryl's death for April to find her identity: "'My people, our people' and met them. The denial had been lifted from my spirit. It was tragic that it had taken Cheryl's death to bring me to accept my identity. But no, Cheryl had once said, 'All life dies to give new life.' Cheryl had died. But for Henry Lee and me, there would be a tomorrow. And it would be better. I would strive for it. For my sister and her son. For my parents. For my people.'" (228).

In *Halfbreed*, Maria Campbell lays bare the history of the Métis. She documents the Halfbreed's state of utter poverty: "The majority of white settlers didn't want violence and withdrew their support after Duck Lake treaty but the Indians, who were starving because of Ottawa's broken promises, supported Dumont and Riel. Poundmaker and Big Bear, Chiefs renowned as warriors and respected throughout the Territories, brought their warriors to join forces with the Halfbreeds." (5) Themes such as corruption of Native leaders through government money occur throughout the novel.

> Louis Riel was hanged in November of 1885.
>
> Charge: high treason.
>
> Gabriel Dumont and a handful of men escaped to Montana.
>
> Poundmaker and Big Bear surrendered and were charged with treason, and sentenced to jail for three years.
>
> The other Halfbreeds escaped to the empty pockets of North Saskatchewan. The total cost to the federal government to stop the Rebellion was $5,000,000. (6)

The halfbreeds who have been living on the land for a long-time face new government regulations which require them to work at the land for three years before being able to claim it. The halfbreeds fought this legislation and fought for the right to stay on the land that they called home. However, the Canadian government overpowered them with thousands of soldiers and they lost the right to hold onto their land. Many families tried to set up a homestead in order to claim some land. 'The land was ten dollars for a quarter sections. Ten acres had to be broken in three years, along with improvement, before title would be granted. Otherwise the land was confiscated by Land Improvement District authorities. Due to the depression and shortage of fur there was no money to buy the implements to break the land.' (7-8)

Some of Campbell's great grandparents fought for the halfbreeds' right to keep the land on which they had been living when the government tried to give it to white settlers. The government was successful in taking away halfbreed land and created a land act which required that a family work on the land to a certain standard to keep it. 'Great Grandma Campbell, whom I always called 'Cheechum,' was a nice Gabriel Dumont and her whole family fought beside Riel and Dumont during the Rebellion. She often told me stories of the Rebellion and the halfbreed people' (11).

Campbell's widowed grandmother tried to get a homestead, but due to poverty and a variety of other circumstances was unable to. Her father was very poor and married her mother who came from a relatively wealthy family. The author establishes through examples that the government discriminates against halfbreeds through policies such as the land act and that whites in the community look down on halfbreeds. The author also shows that while the halfbreeds are poor, they demonstrate a great deal of love for each other in their families and in their community. "All our people were Roman Catholic, but at that time we had neither a priest nor a church. Mom was happy when the Germans built their Church. They were Seventh-Day Adventists and worshipped on Saturday. She wasn't pleased with this but overlooked it; sure that God would understand and forgive her for attending. The important thing was to go to church." (28)

Religion and superstition played an important role in Campbell's upbringing.

> I listened to these stories and asked Cheechum to explain what I did not understand. Many native people practised medicine. The men used it on their traplines so they would have good hauls. They would also go onto other people's lines and take their fur. No one dared to fight back. They could cast spells and even kill with it. They used it on each other sometimes after fights, and they could catch any man or woman they wanted with special love spells. (44)

Maria went to residential school where she wasn't allowed to speak Cree. The community gets their own school. 'School wasn't too bad--Heaven compared to the Residential School. We had a lot of fights with the white kids, but finally, after beating them soundly, we were left alone. There were many remarks made but we learned to ignore or accept them as time went on' (49). There is a unity in the Christmas celebration in a halfbreed community. 'After the ceremony we would all go to the biggest house in the community where the women would have the food all ready. For two days there would be feasting and dancing and laughter' (57-58).

Maria experiences hunting along with her mother and funerals in a halfbreed community. 'Mom and I would take the 22and shoot partridges, ducks and whatever we could get. Mom was a terrible hunter but Daddy had trained me well' (61). So many incidents occurred in which the policies of the government discriminate against halfbreeds. Maria's father gets involved in politics hoping to make life better for halfbreed people. Cheechum was happy with his decision for the betterment of the community.

However, after the halfbreed leaders sold out for the first-time white men inviting halfbreed to their homes, and Maria observed that white man and halfbreed were riding home together in their cars and laughing and drinking like bothers, for the first-time white men had talked to them like men. She became hopeless about the future. In that summer Grannie Campbell died with cancer and she asked for Daddy. Mom was often sick she was hospitalized for three months and she became pregnant she came along with a baby. Daddy realized that he not only destroying his life but also the family, but it is too late. Mom died in the hospital; I have to take care of little brothers and sisters. 'Maria, you are the oldest one and now you have to help me. Momma died this afternoon' (78).

Maria's mother dies, leaving Maria to be the primary caregiver to her younger brothers and sisters. Life is hard in the year after her mother dies. The family moves to a new community in the hope of avoiding the relief people who may take the children away and starting a better life. Grannie Dubuque stays with them for a while to help with the chores and children. Maria's new friend Karen and Maria experience their first romantic crush. Grannie and the family members are shocked to know about Maria's pregnancy. Grannie smiled and said 'Now I know that you belong to me. Don't let anyone tell you that anything is impossible because if you believe honestly in your heart that there's something better for you, then it will all come true. Go out there and find what you want and take it but always remember who you are and why you want it' (97).

Looking after the children interferes with Maria's education. She took them to school for one month but when the teacher found out, she got warning from the school. Then Maria's father took in a common-law wife, Sarah, to help him with the children and chores so that Maria could get education. Maria also met a love interest in Smoky. At last, Maria married Darrell in the hope of saving her brothers and sisters from the relief people. It is fine during the first few months of marriage. One day Darrell lost his job and started drinking; he also started beating Maria. Maria gave birth to a baby girl Lisa. One night, he told her that it was he who had called the relief people to take away her younger brothers and sisters.

Maria moves in with her husband's sister. Things don't go well and Maria and her husband separate. Maria tries to make it on her own but struggles with racism in her employment and love life. She moves to a poor and filthy part of Vancouver to try to make her marriage with Darrel work. Darrel takes Maria to a party where she meets Lil. Eventually, Maria turns to a life of prostitution in order to survive with Lil as her pimp. Maria witnesses another prostitute die of an overdose and the complete lack of caring that others expressed over the woman's death.

Maria realized that she was trapped in the life of prostitution; so she became the keep of a wealthy man, and then realized that that was pretty much the same thing as prostitution. She becomes addicted to hard drugs. Maria meets Ray who helps her kick her addictions and provides her with an income by being a drug mule. Maria saves up enough money to move to Calgary with her daughter; however, in Calgary she struggles with financial troubles and drug addiction; so she moves back to Vancouver and puts her daughter back into a covenant. Ray gets arrested but leaves Maria with enough money to last for a few months. Maria moves to Alberta to work on a ranch and is hired on the condition that she stays out of trouble. The workers at the ranch say disparaging things about Native people until they realize that Maria is Native. Ghosts from Maria's past come to the ranch and Maria worries that they'll impact her employment. Maria moves to Calgary so that she can work and go to school. She faces a difficult paradox: she's going to school in hope of increasing her income, however, she has to work while going to school and she works so much in order to survive that her school work suffers. Maria also copes with an unexpected pregnancy and struggles with the choice of wearing a 'welfare blanket.' Maria falls in love with David while working in the restaurant. And she remembers what Cheechum had told her. 'Someday, somewhere, you'll meet a man who'll grow old with you and you'll know him when you meet him.' (160)

Maria moves to Northern Alberta with David and has a wonderful relationship with him. Maria's former pimp, Lil, is arrested and Maria worries that David will find out about her history. Maria's concern creates problems in their marriage as she struggles with the stress of keeping a secret. Maria turns to her addiction and her marriage suffers. Maria is committed to an institution as her paranoia and addictions get out of hand. Maria also finds support through her friend Trixie who helps her examine her stereotypes about Aboriginal people and her own behaviour. Maria meets Aboriginal activists. She experiences sexism in the Indian movement. Initially Aboriginal activists inspire her but she is soon disappointed. She visits her old community and finds it worse than it was when she left. She met Aboriginal activists and was excluded because she was a woman. Maria assesses contemporary issues in Aboriginal politics and Canadian society.

Maria, inspired by an Aboriginal female activist, begins to educate herself on Aboriginal history in Canada. Maria is employed in a research project on Aboriginal people. The research that she thought would help people actually turns out to be part of a devious plan by the government to further marginalize Aboriginal people. Maria reflects on the welfare blanket metaphor. 'The years of searching, loneliness and pain are over for me. Cheechum said, 'You'll find yourself, and you'll find brothers and sisters. I have brothers and sisters, all over the country. I no longer need my blanket to survive.' (184)

Indigenous Feminism

Indigenous Feminism is a political, social and cultural movement and theory that seeks equality and sovereignty for Indigenous people globally. It is a branch of feminist theory and practice that advocates not just equally with men, but with the decolonization of Indigenous men and women. Indigenous feminism developed out of a need to define the complexities that arise for Indigenous women (and men) as a result of the intersections of race, ethnicity and gender. For example, Indigenous feminism acknowledges the devastating consequences of colonization on Indigenous peoples. The need to define an Indigenous feminism resulted from the need to address various forms of structural oppression experienced by Indigenous people around the world. Indigenous feminism may go by other (geographically specific) names such as: Native American Feminism and Tribal Feminism in North America or Aboriginal Feminism in Australia, but each of these regionally-adapted terms fall under the rubric of Indigenous feminism. Indigenous feminism in practice can be seen in such protest movements as Idle No More, for example.

Before colonization, American Indian women shared a significant role within their communities. Paula Gunn Allen (Laguna Pueblo) argues: "for millennia American Indians have based their social systems, however diverse, on ritual, spirit-centred, woman-focused world-views." Andrea Smith has noted that many Indigenous women argue 'that feminism is actually an indigenous concept that has been co-opted by white women.' This sentiment is echoed elsewhere. Kim Anderson argues that "we now call feminism—which the Merriam Webster's online dictionary defines as 'the theory of political, economic and social equality of the sexes'—was simply a way of life to our ancestors" (82). Paula Gunn Allen's 'Who Is Your Mother? Red Roots of White Feminism,' notes that Native peoples are traditionally feminist and that reclaiming those roots would be empowering to participate in Indigenous decolonization.

However, after colonization, many Indigenous communities were drastically changed. The introduction of patriarchal systems of oppression forced a significant shift in Indigenous women's rights. Kim Anderson writes: "the Europeans who first arrived in Canada were shocked by the position of Aboriginal women in their respective societies. It was not long before they realized that, in order to dominate the land and the people that were occupying it, they needed to disempower the women. Indigenous systems that allocated power to women were incompatible with the kind of colonial power dynamics that would be necessary to maintain colonial power." Additionally, "while women's traditional roles in Indigenous communities vary widely, colonization has reordered gender relations to subordinate women, regardless of their pre-contact status."

Indigenous women continue to face poverty and violence. While both issues are of significant importance to mainstream feminists, Indigenous femenists argue that the effects of colonization make these often very urgent issues for Indigenous women. For example, while varied among North and South American Indigenous communities, concepts of property ownership extended to both men and women. Indigenous women were often property owners, or at least shared in the economic and property ownership opportunities in their communities. After colonization, however, many of these domains were taken away from Indigenous women and given to (Indigenous) men. This, in turn, often placed Indigenous women in precarious positions that ran the risk of poverty, and behind that a heightened risk of violence.

The development of Indigenous feminism came out of a

counter-insurgency against the attempt to apply western feminism equally and effectively to all women regardless of their experiences. Such attempts are seen as fruitless because it homogenized the very diverse experiences of women. As many argue, Indigenous women's experiences with gender are often closely linked to their experiences with race and vice versa, so that an Indigenous woman must address both gender and racial oppression. Andrea Smith has argued that 'all oppressions are related and reinforce each other.'

As a result, Indigenous feminism is connected to Postcolonial feminism. That is to say, the roots of Indigenous feminism are in those of the mainstream feminist movement; however, it also seeks to incorporate specifically Indigenous perspectives into that feminist framework, for example, by contesting the homogeneity of the category "woman" in order to disrupt the 'image of the white middle-class woman as the universal woman.'

Indigenous feminism diverges from postcolonial feminism, however, because some have argued that postcolonial theory in general has largely ignored the histories of colonialism as it exists for Indigenous populations. Some other Indigenous scholars like Robert Warrior, Elizabeth Cook-Lynn, Craig S. Womack have expressed concern over the limits of postcolonial theory and its application to Indigenous studies. There is often distrust of Western theoretical paradigms which can marginalize Indigenous perspectives. There is also significant debate about what constitutes 'post'colonial. As a result, many have moved to Indigenous feminism as a way to redress these issues with postcolonial feminism.

Cheryl Suzack and Shari M. Huhndorf have argued: "Although Indigenous feminism is a nascent field of scholarly inquiry, it has arisen from histories of women's activism and culture that have aimed to combat gender discrimination, secure social justice for Indigenous women, and counter their social erasure and marginalization—endeavours that fall arguably under the rubric of feminism, despite Indigenous women's fraught relationship with the term and with mainstream feminist movements."

Much of Indigenous feminism has taken shape around issues that resulted from colonial practices. It is a direct result of and a direct answer to the colonization and continued oppression of Indigenous peoples around the world. The need to question cultural practices from within allows Indigenous women to actively shape their own communities and helps encourage self-determination and cultural ownership.

Similarly, Indigenous feminism is set apart from other Indigenous rights movements, such as Indigenous liberation theory, because those theories have 'not been attentive to the gendered ways in which colonial oppression and racism function for men and women, or to the inherent and adopted sexisms that some communities manifest.'

There are some within Indigenous communities who choose not to identify as feminist and therefore distance themselves from the mainstream feminism. There are many reasons for this choice. Kim Anderson argues that if Western feminism is unpalatable because it is about rights rather than responsibilities, then we should all take responsibility seriously and ask if we are being responsible to 'all' members of our societies. If we are to reject equality in favour of difference, then we need to make sure that those differences are embedded in systems that empower all members. If we see feminism as being too invested in Western liberalism and individual autonomy, then we need to ensure that our collectivist approaches serve everyone in the collective. And if we want to embrace essential elements of womanhood that have been problematic for Western feminists . . . then we have to ensure that these concepts don't get stuck in literal or patriarchal interpretations.

Many scholars and activists identify Indigenous feminism as occupying the more 'radical' side of the feminist spectrum since it often advocates for an upheaval of all systems of power that organize the subjugation of Indigenous women based on both male supremacy and racial difference. Unlike the more extreme radical feminists, however, Indigenous feminism encourages male participation in the abolition of the 'isms' that result in the logic of domination (see Andrea Smith). Others also speak about the benefits of Indigenous feminism for all Indigenous people. Myrna Cunningham (Miskita) has stated: 'The struggle of Indigenous peoples is not a threat to our struggles as Indigenous women. On the contrary, we see these struggles as reciprocal.'

There has been significant resistance to adopting a westernized, mainstream feminist approach to Indigenous rights and self-determination. The most significant criticism of mainstream feminism has been its marginalization of minorities and lack of racial diversity.

While Indigenous women may acknowledge that there is overlap in the goals of Indigenous feminists and mainstream feminists, many like Celeste Liddle (Arrernte) 'strongly believe that as Aboriginal women, whilst our fights are related to ongoing feminist struggles within other racially marginalized groups, they are not the same.' One such example of the need to incorporate uniquely Indigenous perspectives is in the second wave's struggle for wage parity with their male counterparts. Celeste Liddle argues: 'For example, whilst equal pay is important for all of us, for many years Aboriginal people were historically not paid for their labour at all.' Therefore, the second wave's fight for wage equality (among other issues), was perceived to push the rights of Indigenous women to the periphery.

Another such example is in the length of time to achieve certain rights. For example, while white women deemed to be citizens of Canada were granted the right to vote in 1918, many other women were not allowed the right to vote until much later. Aboriginal women in Canada were not allowed to vote until the 1960s, at which time the second wave of feminism had moved away from such issues. Rauna Kuokkanen (Sami) has argued for an Indigenous paradigm, because while "some feminist theories and practices also aim at social and political changes in a society, . . . their approaches often exclude notions of collectivity as well as land rights which are central elements for Indigenous peoples." The criticism against mainstream feminism is synthesized by Cunningham who argues:

> They see that the dominant feminist paradigm is based on an unacknowledged model of centre and periphery. In this model, Indigenous, African-descendent and poor women occupy the periphery and must accept the ideas and conceptualization of feminism as defined by those at the centre. In other words, we Indigenous women are expected to accept the dominant picture of what constitutes women's oppression and women's liberation. The trouble is, this picture is only a partial match with our own experiences. Elements of our experience that do not match this picture are denied or marginalized. This dominant model tries to homogenize the women's movement, claiming that all women have the same demands and the same access to the enjoyment of their rights. This flawed assumption denies the diverse cultural, linguistic and social needs and visions of distinct groups of women.

Survival has been a significant issue for all Indigenous peoples and many have suggested that feminist discourse should take second place to the goal of survival (of people, culture, language). Andrea Smith, as well as many others, have argued that 'since Native women are the women most likely to be killed by domestic violence, they are clearly not surviving. So when we talk about survival of our nations, who are we including?'

Aboriginal feminism (also sometimes referred to as Indigenous feminism) has also taken a different trajectory from the mainstream, white Anglo-Canadian women's movement. Aboriginal women have largely not participated in that movement, in part because Aboriginal women's organizations have focused on issues related to colonialism and cultural discrimination. Further, some Aboriginal women have explicitly rejected the label of 'feminist' because, it is perceived to suggest 'a strongly anti-natal and anti-family stance that is offensive [to Aboriginal women] as they rebuild their nations.' Others have viewed the universal sisterhood associated with the second wave with hostility, perceiving the idea that all women are the same as an erasure of difference and as an attempt at colonization. By and large, Aboriginal women active in pursuing their rights, such as those belonging to the Native Women's Association of Canada, 'do not see themselves as part of a separate feminist movement but rather one that will complement the aboriginal organizations, which tend to be male dominated.'

Aboriginal women have worked together to address gender and cultural discrimination as they experience it. One of the most notable instances of this activism was around the issue of who qualifies as a Status Indian under the Indian Act. The status of 'Indian' was conferred upon persons whose father was a status Indian. According to an amendment to the Act made in 1951, a native man always passed on his status to his wife and children (whether she was Aboriginal or not), while a native woman who married a non-native lost her own status and could not pass on her status to her children. These conditions for qualifying for status caused many women to be displaced from their communities. These amendments inspired activism on the part of the Tobique Women's Group, as well as the founding of the Native Women's Association of Canada in 1973, in order to enable women to achieve equality not only as women, but as Aboriginal women. The struggle for women to receive equal status under the Indian Act was also clear in various challenges to the Act, first by Mary Two-Axe Earley, followed by the human rights challenges raised by Jeannette Lavell, Yvonne Bedard and Sandra Lovelace in the 1970s. In 1985, the Indian Act was amended to address unequal treatment of native women with Bill C-31 which allowed the return of Native Status to those who had lost it.

Other women have also contested the mainstream feminist history of 'waves.' In the case of Black Canadian women, the mainstream history of the first and second waves is problematic insofar as their struggles to enable women to leave their homes and partake in the labour force ignored that certain women had always worked to support their families. Most clear in American Black feminist Soujourner Truth's 'Ain't I a Woman?' speech, the experiences of black women in Canada have not been adequately addressed by conventional feminist histories. Like Aboriginal women, some black feminists have articulated their experiences in terms of a racially disadvantaged struggle for equal treatment, and that their struggle is not only against patriarchy but systemic racism as well.

Black women saw a need to fund their own organizations, including missionary work in the late 19th century through the Women's Home Missionary Society of the Baptist Church. Further, black women founded organizations like the Coloured Women's Club in Montreal (founded in 1900) to expand opportunities for people in the Black community, through mutual support.

The 'double burden' of work and household labour, that would be an important element of feminism in its second wave, had long been present for black women who were also less likely to be paid fairly. While it was middle class white women's experiences during and after WW II, coupled with the emergence of Betty Friedan's *The Feminine Mystique* that led middle-class white women to consider engaging in the workforce, 'by the Second World War at least 80 percent of Black women in Canada worked in the domestic-services sector and earned less than their white counterparts.' Black women in Canada established a national women's organization in the post-war years, with the founding of the Canadian Negro Women's Association in 1951. Though the organization started largely as a social organization, over several decades, it became more activist in orientation; in

1980, after a national conference, it changed its name to the Congress of Black Women to reflect the changing structures and concerns of the organization.

Aboriginal women in Canada frequently experience challenges and discrimination that are not necessarily shared by non-Aboriginal women, or by Aboriginal men. Aboriginal women have been described as facing a 'double burden'—that for being discriminated against as women, and further for being Aboriginal. To begin to understand this situation, and why the circumstances of Aboriginal women deserve their own careful consideration, we must examine how both Native/ non-Native relations and gender relations developed in Canada's colonial history, where these two types of relations intersect or diverge.

As non-Aboriginal settlers first arrived in what is now Canada, they brought with them their patriarchal social codes and beliefs, and tried to make sense of Aboriginal society through a patriarchal lens. As the colonies consolidated to form the Dominion of Canada, Crown policies were created throughout the country with the goal of assimilating and 'civilizing' First Nations peoples based on a European model. These policies had profound effects on Aboriginal women across the country. Outlining these early histories of gender relations gives the reader a sense of how initial colonial assumptions resulted in the drastic alteration of women's influence and social systems in a relatively short time. These impacts continue to be felt by Aboriginal women across Canada today.

Women were respected for their spiritual and mental strength and men were respected for their spiritual and physical strength. Women were given the responsibility of bearing children and were given the strength and power to carry this responsibility. Men had always respected that spiritual and mental strength and women respected the men's physical strength. There was always a balance between men and women as each had their own responsibilities as a man and as a woman. (Beverley Jacobs)

Despite the vast socio-cultural diversity amongst Canada's hundreds of First Nations, historians and experts largely agree that a balance between women and men's roles typically existed in pre-contact Aboriginal societies where women and men had different but complementary roles. Many First Nations were matrilineal, meaning that descent—wealth, power and inheritance—were passed down through the mother.

Historians and scholars have emphasized the various capacities in which women were able to hold positions of power and leadership in their community. Lisa J. Udel, for example, explains that motherhood was honoured and revered as key to the thriving of the culture and was not always strictly defined by its biological role; it was understood as a position of leadership and responsibility for caring for and nurturing others. The role of the Clan Mother is frequently cited as an example of a powerful political role, central to the Haudenosaunee Six Nations confederacy. While many Nations had male chiefs, in some societies such as the Haudeonsaunee, women selected the Chief and were also able to take his power away. Historians and experts emphasize that women across many First Nations were responsible for land holdings and allocation of resources—they controlled access to certain areas as well as distribution of its products.

Ultimately, however, as women's roles varied greatly between First Nations, they shared similar characteristics. Scholar Rebecca Tsosie identifies three common characteristics: gender roles were not ranked hierarchically but were considered complementary; in many cases women were able to transcend gender roles, and 'the central role of Native women within their societies is often reflected in the religious or spiritual content of their cultures.'

Shari M. Huhndorf and Cheryl Suzack point out, 'although Indigenous women do not share a single culture, they do have a common colonial history. The imposition of patriarchy has transformed Indigenous societies by diminishing Indigenous women's power, status and material circumstances.'

For further readings on Aboriginal women's traditional roles, see Paula Gunn Allen's *The Sacred Hoop* and Laura E. Donaldson's '"But we are your mothers, you are our sons': Gender, Sovereignty, and the Nation in Early Cherokee Women's Writing" in *Indigenous Women and Feminism: Politics, Activism, Culture* (Vancouver: UBC Press, 2010, 43-55).

As settlers arrived in what is now North America, they brought with them a foreign patriarchal European value system. European settlers imposed their own frameworks of understanding onto Aboriginal social systems which had particular ramifications for Aboriginal women. As Julia V. Emberley describes, settlers made sense of Aboriginal societies by viewing them through a European, patriarchal lens, assuming that Victorian principles represented the natural order of things. For instance, many settlers held onto Victorian beliefs that women were delicate and ill-equipped for hard labour, and thus viewed Aboriginal women who worked the land as proof that Aboriginal men treated women as inferior, for they were doing the men's work. The power and agency of Aboriginal women were invisible to them.

Laura E. Donaldson provides another telling example of Eurocentric mischaracterization. She describes the Cherokee role of Ghigau, or 'war woman,' a figure who was known as 'the most beloved woman' after she reached menopause: "The Ghigau sat in council meetings with both the peace and war chiefs, decided the fate of war captives, prepared the purgative Black Drink at the centre of many Cherokee ceremonies, and led the women's council. In his Diary of the American Indians, which was published originally in 1755, James Adair derided this unique political institution as a petticoat government—a direct jab, according to Paula Gunn Allen at the power of the Ghigau. Indeed, Allen argues that the honour accorded her by the Cherokee people offended the Euro-American belief in universal male dominance."

European men further believed that a woman should remain chaste and 'virtuous,' according to their cultural and religious beliefs. Settlers developed and held onto the mythical archetype of the virtuous Indian Princess willing to reject her own people for Christian civilization. Thus developed the Indian Princess/ Squaw dichotomy, what Rayna Green terms 'the Pocahontas perplex,' placing Aboriginal women into a restrictive binary based on European patriarchal values. If a woman could not be virtuous by strict Victorian standards which, as Green points out, was nearly impossible, she was deemed unworthy of respect. These concepts were written right into the Indian Act, with certain rights afforded to men and women of 'good moral character,' as determined by the Indian agent. The Indian agent became, therefore, a sort of sexual policing agent. Indian agents had the power to act as justices of the peace or magistrates, giving them legal authority to monitor and control their Indian charges. Any sexual relations that did not conform to monogamy in marriage were seen as un-civilized and counter to the government's civilizing mission. Joan Sangster points out that female sexuality was regulated in numerous ways, with colonial law as 'one crucial site of sexual regulation.' The Indian Act gave the agent power to jail people, and the agent's responsibility for registering births, marriages, and those eligible for Indian status gave agents power to punish those who did not conform. While many First Nations customary laws allowed divorce, Indian agents forbade them. A woman cohabitating with a new partner could be charged with bigamy and sent off to a reformatory, far from her family and homeland. As Sangster points out, The fact that the Indian Affairs filing system designated a whole category for 'Immorality on the Reserves,' with almost all the complaints centering on sexual misbehavior, indicates the importance of the agent's role as custodian of sexual morality.

The Juvenile Delinquents Act and Training School Act of the 1950s, for example, were established to train young women away from perceived 'promiscuity' and into domesticity, forcing European patriarchal roles onto Native women. If Native women did not recognize or obey European patriarchal roles, they could be severely punished. While written legislation provided standards for behaviour, day-to-day experiences did not always reflect these laws. Although there are consistent threads of resistance, some aspects of colonial laws and ideals filtered into First Nations communities and individual mentalities, including gender roles and sexual relations. Sangster draws upon sociologist Karen Anderson to explain that the internalization of these sexual double-standards, 'reorder the domestic sphere on reserves 'involved both direct coercion and the indirect 'colonization of the soul,' with the colonized literally coming to discipline themselves.' As such, legal ramifications occasionally became weapons used by community members who wrote to the Indian Agent, or directly to Ottawa, to complain about 'sexual deviancy.' This history has led to contemporary ideas of Aboriginal women's sexuality. As Lubicon Cree scholar Robyn Bourgeois described in an interview, the myth of the Aboriginal woman as a sexual deviant persists in contemporary Canadian society with some very real ramifications: "No, this view hasn't changed, and yes it is something I have encountered. The myth of the deviant Aboriginal woman continues to plague us, reinforced by dominant cases that coalesce prostitution and Aboriginal women into a single entity. Contemporary Canadian society dismisses violence against Aboriginal women and girls today on the basis of these perceived deviances (addicted, sexually available). We are not even treated as human beings. Human beings have the right to a life free from violence, yet we have to convince the Canadian state to step up and protect us. And these stereotypes provide the justification for why the State doesn't step up."

Having explored the ways in which colonial ideas perpetuated discrimination against Aboriginal women, it is important to understand the ways in which these ideas have been retained to the present day. This discrimination continues to be reinforced through various means, perhaps most notably the Indian Act. As such, we will explore three areas of gender discrimination which the Indian Act continues to perpetuate and normalize: regulation of the family, the reserve system and geographic exclusion, and political exclusion. Government policy and legislation impacted the expected roles and rights of Aboriginal women in various and far-reaching ways. The Indian Act is only one of such policies, yet is the most common critique raised by scholars who point out how women were excluded from positions of power. The Indian Act remains a central feature in the lives of Aboriginal women, and is essential to understanding the current and historical socio-political situation in Canada.

The Indian Act, created by the federal government in 1876, was evidently designed with the colonial ideal of men as leaders and heads of households and women as dependents of their husbands. The Indian Act denied women the right to possess land and marital property—only widows could possess land under the reserve system. However, a widow could not inherit her husband's personal property upon his death—everything, including the family house, legally went to his children. Government agents modified the Act slightly in 1884, with an amendment that allowed men to will their estate to their wives, but a wife could only receive it if the Indian agent determined she was of 'good moral character.' This particular amendment remained in the Indian Act until 1951, although to this day men still hold exclusive rights to property, even if a relationship ends. This has far-reaching implications in the lives and safety of the affected women: Over the years more and more women were being thrown out of their homes by husbands. While the men then moved their girlfriends—often [non-status]—into the family home, the Indian women and children had to move into condemned houses or in with relatives who already were overcrowded. Since the Indian Act gave men sole ownership of property through certificates of possession, women had no housing rights or recourse to help through the law.

The European belief that the patriarchal, nuclear family was a natural means of organization influenced settler-Aboriginal relationships. Many First Nations historically have operated on a matrilineal system where descent is traced through the mother, meaning that a child would become a member of his or her mother's clan. Many societies were also matrilocal, in which a man married into a woman's family and would live with her community, resulting in settlement patterns based on the female line. In contrast, European settlers had taken for granted that a family was structured with men as the head of the family and the women as subservient, and tried to understand Aboriginal families by imposing a patriarchal European family model onto matriarchal Aboriginal kinship systems. This belief was perpetuated throughout government policies that attempted to restructure the Aboriginal family to fit this mould. Aboriginal kinship systems were forcibly restructured over time through a number of policies, including the Indian Act, Indian status, and the residential school system. Scholars, community members and other experts point out that even after the closure of residential schools, foster parenting, adoptions [link to 60s scoop], and other child welfare policies continue to separate Aboriginal families and place them in non-Aboriginal homes and kinship systems.

Aboriginal families initially continued to recognize their own matriarchal descent patterns and matrilocal systems despite encroaching non-Aboriginal settlement. In 1851, however, this would be forcibly disrupted when the government created legislation to determine who qualified as Indian. The government decided that to be an Indian, one had to be an Indian male, be the child of an Indian male, or be married to an Indian male. Under this system, a woman depended on her relationship with a man to determine whether or not she was an Indian. This completely contradicted the matrilineal system of many First Nations and disrupted a hereditary system that had been in place for hundreds of generations.

Those who qualified as Indian under this legislated criteria would gain Indian 'status,' hence the term Status or Non-Status Indian. For women, status was not guaranteed. Legislation stated that a status Indian woman who married a non-Indian man would cease to be an Indian. She would lose her status, and with it, she would lose treaty benefits, health benefits, the right to live on her reserve, the right to inherit her family property and even the right to be buried on the reserve with her ancestors. However, if an Indian man married a non-native woman, he would keep all his rights. His wife would in fact gain Indian status. Even if an Indian woman married another Indian man, she would cease to be a member of her own band and would become a member of his. If a woman was widowed, or abandoned by her husband, she would become enfranchised and lose status and her rights altogether.

Alternatively, if a non-native woman married an Indian man, she would gain status. In all these situations, a woman's status was entirely dependent on her husband. As is explicitly stated in Section 12 (1) (b) of the Indian Act, 'a woman who married a person who is not an Indian. . . [is] not entitled to be registered.'

As Emberley explains, the exclusion of women and devaluing of their status established "fraternal links between aboriginal and colonial men, created fissures within aboriginal families along gender lines, and eventually led to patriarchal relations and the regulating of 'the aboriginal family' on a European bourgeois model." Once the Indian Act was passed, the responsibilities of men and women changed drastically. As a result of being confined to a reserve, the traditional men and women lost their responsibilities in using their strengths, either physically or mentally. Women were thought of as property by our O:gwe ho:we men who became acculturated into believing that they had to think like white men. The entitlement to status under the Indian

Act itself enabled that to happen wherein the male would gain status and his wife and his children would gain his status. Jacobs

In the 21st century, violence against Aboriginal women and girls has increasingly taken centre stage even as a cascade of evidence, especially after the 1989 Montreal massacre, roused the mainstream women's movement. Revelations associated with serial killers John Martin Crawford in Saskatchewan (convicted 1996; Goulding) and Robert Pickton in BC (convicted 2007; BC Missing Women Commission of Inquiry) underscored violence as a special issue for indigenous activists but many earlier murders, such as that of Cree twenty-year-old Helen Betty Osborne, in The Pas, Manitoba, in 1971, supplied ample proof of historic victimization.

Although laughter greeted a feminist MP, NDPer Margaret Mitchell, in 1982 when she raised the question of violence in the House of Commons, Canadians increasingly condemned its prevalence. In 1991, Brian Mulroney's Conservative government appointed the Canadian Panel on Violence against Women in a tactic widely regarded as an effort to seize an embarrassing issue from NWAC, the National Action Committee on the Status of Women and mainstream feminist critics of state inaction. 'The glaring absence of specific communities of women' from Panel membership confirmed a rift between Ottawa and the organized women's movements with their demands for action (Gotell 56). While women of colour, immigrant women and women with disabilities remained largely ignored, Aboriginal women secured "the addition of four 'Aboriginal Circle' members, chosen by and responsible to their organizations" (Gotell 57). Such last-minute inclusion reflected emerging public recognition of the particular plight of Indigenous women.

Ultimately, despite its boycott by many anti-violence activists, the Panel's report 'reflected feminist discourses and approaches,' notably in its emphasis on violence as 'shaped by complex and intersecting inequalities' (Gotell 58, 60) and the necessity of broad social change. The Conservative government publicly 'embraced' much of the report 'but refused to commit any new budgetary resources to the battle against violence' (Gotell 68). In 1993, the federal victory of the Chrétien Liberals, with their own law and order agenda and emphasis on cutbacks to transfer payments, made little difference. Anti-violence work by NWAC, as with other groups, continued to depend on uncertain and conditional state funding. Even when the 2000 Report of the Royal Commission on Aboriginal Peoples and 2015 Report of the Truth and Reconciliation Commission presented incontrovertible evidence of historic violence, amounting in effect to cultural genocide, governments remained reluctant partners.

The on-going revelation of Canada's 'missing and murdered' Indigenous women nevertheless kept violence in the public spotlight. In 2003, NWAC president Terri Brown, of B.C.'s Tahitian Nation, built on decades of anti-violence work by Aboriginal women's groups to publicly condemn the estimated 'more than 500 Aboriginal women gone missing' over two decades. Calling for immediate action, she 'underscored the limited investigation' into such tragedies (Sterritt). A year later NWAC launched its Sisters in Spirit (SIS) initiative, which included a campaign asking Ottawa for $10 million to fund research. In 2005, shortly before its defeat, Paul Martin's Liberal government announced that it would provide $5 million over five years.

That funding, continued by the Harper minority government, allowed NWAC to initiate a long-needed database on the missing and murdered. In March 2010, SIS published *What Their Stories Tell Us*. This set out the critical knowledge gaps, including lack of attention to the ethnicity of victims and injurious stereotypes, as keys to the recurring failure to tackle systematically the abuse of girls and women (Crowder). The Harper government, which, equally revealingly of its attitude to data, abolished the long census in June 2010, at first seemed indifferent.

Conclusion

The invaluable service rendered by First Nations writers and Feminist organizations is making First Nations visible. After centuries of denial and denigration, the First nations of Canada have become powerful enough to make their voices heard, and are fighting to establish their identity in the Europe-dominated society. During the second quarter of the 20th century, the First Nations were looked upon as a vanishing race. The trend has reversed now. By the 1990s, they became independent of the tactics of the Indian agents who always had stifled their voice. It is an indubitable fact that most First Nations people in Canada desire a peaceful and harmonious life. The tears and bloodshed of the past years' resistance attest to their attempts of survival. It also effects the realization that a peaceful and harmonious existence in a hegemonic system is only a myth.

The settler's attitude towards the First Nations contributed to creating the First Nations problem. The European power structures had tried various tactics to wipe out the traces of First Nations from Canada. At the face of all the suppressions and stifling, the First Nations clung to their culture and now they overtly attempt to establish their culture and identity and resist the injustice and discrimination on them.

The image of the First Nations created by media hype ought to be changed, by portraying reality rather than the fruits of imagination. The First Nations writers are attempting to dispel the negative stereotypes and project objective images. This may help their people move towards the centre from their position of marginality, thus making Canada a pluralist society.

The Europeans have to learn a lot from the First Nations.

This learning will help shatter their perceptions of the First Nations. The First Nations are the owners of thousands of years old heritage. Though the First Nations do not share a homogeneous culture, they share certain fundamental principles of social control. As theirs was an ecofriendly life, they held a deep insight into the entire ecological balance, in sharp contrast to the ethnocentrism of the Europeans. They live in a holistic social context and maintain a reciprocal and harmonious relationship with every element and entity in the universe. When the First Nations lived as a hunting and foraging community, they never hunted any animal beyond their need. The teaching of 'Seventh generation' is gaining momentum now. It means, when the occupants of the earth do anything on earth, they must think of its impact on earth, and how it will affect future generations. Resources should be retained for posterity.

The European settlers regarded First Nations culture and natural insights as uncivilized and pursued their exploitative practices, devastating resources, bringing the land to the brink of an ecological disaster. As going back to the ancient ways of life is not feasible, humans should attempt to incorporate the First Nations' ways to preserve the ecological balance. The 'seventh generation' teaching also demands that people should live in harmony. The recent technological advancement has resulted in the contamination of the earth and atmosphere.

First Nations children were educated with an ecological system perspective which upholds the inter-relatedness of all forms of life on earth. Amidst a host of socio-cultural differences, the First Nations movements succeeded in leading a spiritual and cultural revolution in their lives. Collective awareness is to be developed for the hegemonic control of cultural resources and value systems of the community. United resistance moves and show of strength of the First Nations like demonstration, blockades etc. contributed to the revival of the depressed psyche of the First Nations. In the frequent meetings, they raised their fears and anxieties and sought solutions to the issues perceiving the present and future dynamics of hegemonic and counter hegemonic perspectives on the motives of the government. The First nations are accelerating their resistance activities and offering even violent responses to attract public attention to their problems. The Oka standoff is an example. Though the government successfully crushed the resistance, using police and army, the confrontation received unprecedented national and international attention. To broaden their social support, First Nations organizations attempt to attain more media coverage for their activities. The Indian Treaty Council under the official recognition of the UNO is seeking to alleviate the ills caused in the past. Still they have a long way to go.

The First Nations stick to retention of the Reserve system as an essential base to retain and strengthen their racial and cultural identity. The First Nations, in spite of the fear of imminent losses, uphold their traditional belief that land is gift of the Great Spirit and the resources should be shared regardless of origin or affiliation.

In order to exist in the dominant society, they have to learn the European language, their sciences etc. Simultaneously, they want to perpetuate their own history, culture and medicinal practices. The experience of the past has taught them to view governmental measures with a keen acuity. They are keen on reclaiming their culture, dignity and self-respect.

The First Nations rights are being recognized now in Northern British Columbia; experiment is made by issuing tree-farm-licence to the First Nations bands which had earlier been given to companies only. According to the licence, the licensee has the right to cut and use the wood. He is responsible for the forest area and he has to replant the cut trees. Fishing rights are given to Indians without governmental restrictions. Attempts are being made to revive the communal nature of First Nations life. The First Nations are seeking access to the dominant society alongside their attempts to reclaim their culture. The Euro Canadians' perception of the First Nations and their attempts to 'civilize' them precisely created the Indian problem.

Many Indian communities now attempt to develop the potential of the reserves by constructing shopping malls and services and developing industries towards attaining economic solvency and viability. These measures check the drain of financial resources as well as reduce joblessness among the First Nations people. First Nations cultural centres attempt at the revitalization of their culture and promoting cross-cultural awareness through reciprocal learning and instruction. The exclusionary term Euro-Canadian is no more in official use. However, the terms whites and Euro-Canadians are still used in private circles.

The First Nations of Canada continue their struggle for the actualization of their dream of decolonization. The treaty promises have not been 'honoured.' Still, they are victims of racism. Tribal councils and the Assembly of First Nations should join hands to fight for the realization of the First Nations claim of self-government. In settling many key issues, the Canadian political hierarchy ignores the centrality of the First Nations.

The First Nations are incorporating their traditional knowledge along with modern technology to regain control over their lives and economies and developing a holistic ecosystem.

The increasing number of Third World writers and scholars in the Western World has projected the issues of Third World countries. Much of the socialist criticism is focused on the problems of Third World countries. The concept of Europe as a self-contained entity is being deconstructed and the place of English literature is being challenged. The colonized were manoeurved as the colonizers/ imperialist inferior 'other' to affirm their hegemony by imposing identities through dichotomizing images of representation, with positive codes on the colonizers and negative codes on the colonized. The East/ West, Orient/ Occident binaries are no more tenable to the Third World countries.

Though First Nations form less than four percent of Canadian population, they stick together as members of a collective which gives them added political strength. Today First Nations are not isolated from white societies. Since the period of European ingression into the Americas, the lives of the First Nations have undergone multifarious changes. Although the effects of colonisation still persist, the First Nations are attempting to rebuild their nation and establish their identity.

The economic sector of the First Nations has shifted from the hunting and foraging to the industries. Greater political autonomy and traditional ecological knowledge are advantageous to the industrial development, providing educational and employment opportunities. Programmes like Self Improvement through Empowerment (SITE) introduced by Chief Wesley are aimed at the improvement of the conditions of First Nations people. The programme has a holistic approach to life. It begins with improving the individual which in turn improves the family and community at large. Recuperation of the cultural activities and traditional practices define the spirit of the First Nations and strengthen their sense of identity.

The ridiculing of the First Nations' religious practices during the onslaught of colonization had effected setbacks in the First Nations' therapies. However its acceptance and recognition in the contemporary society has helped a lot in reviving it. Reexamination of First Nations' medical practices in modern scientific terms proves its effectiveness.

The annual conference held by the Crow Agency upheld the culture and heritage of the First Nations and attempts their revival. The Indian rituals and ceremonies of the past were performed in these conferences for the spiritual revitalization and cultural unity of the communities. Though the Europeans attempted to impose their culture and religion on the First Nations, the First Nations cultures persisted and its value is being discovered by the invaders.

The revitalization of the First Nations traditions and values are sought to solve many of the evils associated with First Nations life in the contemporary society. The First Nations healing practices are being revitalized with the passage of the 1978 Freedom of Religion Act. The reinstation of First Nations shamans and healers has started the revival of First Nations values.

Feminists challenge the traditional concept of family relations. Traditional ideologies of marriage push women into marriage where they find themselves tied to domestic and parental responsibilities. Unequal power relations of sexes often erupt violence and abuse. Separation and divorce also complicate family forms. The changing concept of family structures necessitates gender equality in the family. Still women are discarding their traditional role as homemaker and participating in the labour force. At the turn of the century, the concept of family has received diverse connotations. Lone parent families are on the increase. Massive economic and social changes in the contemporary period bring women in the labour force resulting in their independence of male support.

As Indians' struggles gained momentum, newspapers began cashing in on sensationalizing the resistance movement. The press reports always perverted the truth about the statements and activities of the activists. Jeannette Armstrong exemplifies a lot of such cases through the exegesis of the experience of her character Slash.

The First Nations have recognized and retained their traditional skills like hunting, trapping etc. and utilizes its application in advanced industries and technology. Biological diversity research developing in Canada is applying the tools provided by the First Nations knowledge and ecology. The industrially advanced countries of the West are now turning to the seventh-generation teachings of the First Nations people to retain ecological balance to live in harmony with nature.

One of the enabling outcomes of postcolonialism is that the

binarism of East and West are no more tenable. Blame exists that the trend towards the reclamation of First Nations history and culture is not meant to atone for past sins but to claim a past for the settler community. Colonialism's insidious effects cannot be easily eradicated completely since they get complicated with other kinds of cultural domination coexistent with colonialism. Although most of the formal colonies do not endure external political control, covert impositions of hegemony still exist in the form of economic and political pressure.

The emergence of neo-imperialisms is directly linked to European colonialism. Many colonized nations like America emerged powerful after gaining freedom from the imperial centre. Such powers impose their hegemony under the masks of political support, economic and military aid and advice. The Caribbean countries' dependence of development bring them under the neo-imperialistic strategy of the United States. The United States' hegemony is manifest in the cultural economic sphere of world nations. European aid and advice generously provided to Third World countries like Afghanistan implicitly perpetuate Euroculture in these regions.

The First Nations cultures of America had accorded respect for all beings on earth. Ecofeminism develops a polemic against the Europeanisation of Third World countries and imitation of European culture that devastates the ecology.

Bibliography

Adams, Howard. *Prison of Grass: Canada from a Native Point of View*. Saskatoon: Fifth House, Rpt.,1989.

Allen, Paula Gunn, ed. *Spider Woman's Granddaughters: Traditional tales and Contemporary Writing by Native American Women*. Boston: Beacon, 1989.

_____. *The Sacred Hoop*. Boston: Beacon Press, 1986.

Anderson, Benedict. *Imagined Communities: Reflections on the Origin and Spread of Nationalism*. London: Verso, 1983.

Armstrong, Jeannette. *Slash*. Rev. ed. Penticton, BC: Theytus, 1990.

_____. *Whispering in Shadows*. Penticton, BC: Theytus, 2000.

_____, 'Racism: Racial Exclusivity and Cultural Supremacy,' *Give Back: First Nations Perspectives on Cultural Practice*, ed. Caffyn Kelley. North Vancouver. Gallerie Pub, 1922.

_____. 'The Disempowerment of First North American Native Peoples and Empowerment through Their Writing,' *An Anthology of Canadian Literature in Native English*, ed. Daniel David Mouses and Terry Goldie, Oxford: University of Oxford Press, 1992.

Ashcroft, Bill, Gareth Griffiths and Helen Tiffin. *Postcolonial Studies*. London and New York: Routledge, 2000.

_____. *Key Concepts in Postcolonial Studies*. London and New York: Routledge, 1998.

Ashok, A.V. *Narrative: A Student's Companion*. Chennai: T.R., 1998.

Atwood, Margaret. *Survival: A Thematic Guide to Canadian Literature*. Concord: Anansi, 1991.

Awatere, Donna. *Maori Sovereignty*. Auckland: Broadsheet, 1984.

Bakhtin, M.M. and Medvedev P.M. *The Formal Method of Literary Scholarship*. Cambridge: Harvard University Press, 1985.

Barker, Francis, ed. *Europe and Its Others*. Colchester: University of Essex, 1985.

Basu, Amrita. ed. *Women's Movement in Global Perspective*. New Delhi: Kali for women, 1995.

Bennet, Tony. *Outside Literature*. London: Routledge, 1990.

Berkhofer, Robert F. *The White Man's Indian: Images of the American Indian from Columbus to the Present*. New York: Vintage, 1979.

Bhabha, Homi K. *Nation and Narration*. London: Routledge, 1990.

_____. *The Location of Culture*. London: Routledge, 1994.

Broome, Richard. *Aboriginal Australians: Black Responses to White Dominance. 1788-1994*. St. Leonards: Allen & Unwin, 1994.

Brown, Russel. 'Can a Postmodern Nation Have a Tradition? An Investigation into the English-Canadian Literary Tradition.' *Journal of Indo-Canadian Studies*, 1, 2 (2001).

Butler, Judith. *Gender Trouble: Feminism and the Subversion of Identity*. New York: Routledge, 1990.

Cameroon, Elspeth, ed. *Canadian Culture: An Introductory Reader*. Toronto: Canadian scholars' Press, 1997.

Campbell, Maria. *Halfbreed*. Toronto: McClelland & Stewart, 1973.

_____. *Stories of the Road Allowance People*. Theytus Books, 1995.

_____ and Linda Griffiths. *The Book of Jessica*. Playwrights Canada Press, 1997.

_____ . *Achimoona*. Fifth House, 1985.

_____ and Peter Campbell. *Little Badger and the Fire Spirit*. McClelland & Stewart, 1980.

_____. and David MacLagan. *Riel's People: How the Metis Lived*. 1976.

_____. *People of the Buffalo: How the Plains Indians Lived*. Firefly Books, 1990.

Cesaire, Aime. *Discourse on Colonialism*. Trans. Joan Pinkam. New York: Monthly Review Press, 1972.

Charles Keil. *Urban Blues*. Chicago: Univ. of Chicago Press, 1966.

Charters, Samuel B. *The Country Blues*. New York: Rinehart, 1959.

Cixous, Helene. 'The Laugh of the Medusa.' *Signs: Journal of Women in Culture and Society*, 1.4 (1976), 875-93.

Clifford, J.E. *The Predicament of Culture*. Cambridge: Harvard Univ. Press, 1998.

Colebrook, Claire. *New Literary Histories: New Historicism and Contemporary Criticism*. Manchester: University Press, 1997.

Crosby, Marcia. 'Construction of the Imaginary Indian,' *Vancouver Anthology: The Institutional Politics of Art*, ed. Stan Douglas. Van-

couver: Talonbooks, 1991.
Culleton, Beatrice. *In Search of April Raintree*. Winnipeg: Pemmican, 1984.
_____. *Spirit of the White Bison*. Winnipeg: Pemmican, 1985.
Curnow, Allen. *Look Back Harder: Critical Writings 1937-1984*, ed. Peter Simpson. Auckland: Auckland University Press, 1987.
Dangle, Arjun, ed. *Poisoned Bread: Translations from Modern Marathi Dalit Literature*. Bombay: Orient Longman, 1994.
Davies, Jack and Hob Hodge. *Aboriginal Writing Today*. Canberra: Australian Institute of Aboriginal Studies, 1985.
Derrida, J. *Of Grammatology*, trans. Gayatri Chakravorty Spivak. Baltimore: John Hopkins University Press, 1976.
Dyck Noel, ed. *Indigenous Peoples and the Nation-State: 'Fourth World' Politics in Canada, Australia and Norway*. St. John: Institute of Social and Economic Research Memorial University of Newfoundland, 1992.
Easthope, Antony. *Poetry as Discourse*. London: Methuen, 1983.
Eco, Umberto. *Misreadings*, trans. William Weaver. London: Jonathan Cape, 1993.
Erdich, Louise. *The Beet Queen*. Toronto: Bantam Books, 1986.
Fanon, F. *Black Skin, White Masks*, trans. Charles Lam Markmann, London: Mac Gibbon and Kee, 1968.
_____. *Towards the African Revolution*, trans. Haaken Chevalier. New York Monthly Review Press, 1967. Orig. 1964, Paris.
Finnegan, Ruth. *Oral Poetry: Its Nature, Significance and Social Context*. Bloomington: Indiana University Press, 1992.
Foucault, M. *Discipline and Punish: The Birth of the Prison*, trans. Alan Sheridan. New York: Longman, 1977.
Francis, Daniel. *The Imaginary Indian: The Image of the Indian in Canadian Culture*. Vancouver: Arsenal Pulp Press, 1997.
Frances Kemble. *Journal of a Residence on a Georgia Plantation in 1838-1839*. New York: Harper, 1863.
Freire, Paulo. *Pedagogy of the Oppressed*, trans. Myra Bergman Ramos. Harmondsworth: Penguin, 1983.
Friesen, John W. *Rediscovering the First Nations of Canada*. Calgary: Detselig Enterprises, 1997.
Gilbert, Kelvin, ed. *Inside Black Australia: An Anthology of Aboriginal*

Poetry. Victoria: Penguin, 1988.

Glass, Colleen and Archie Weller, ed. *Us Fellas: An Anthology of Aboriginal Writing*. Perth: Artlook Books, 1987.

Goldie, Terry. *Fear and Temptation: The Image of the Indigene in Canadian, Australian and New Zealand Literatures*. Kingston: McGill Queen's University Press, 1989.

Goodwin, Ken and Alan Lawson, ed. *The Macmillan Anthology of Australian Literature*. Melbourne: Macmillan, 1990.

Gramsci, Antonio. *Selections from the Prison Notebooks*, trans. Quintin Hoore and Geoffrey N. Smith. Madras: Orient Longman, 1996.

Grant, Agnes, ed. *Our Bit of Truth: An Anthology of Canadian Native Literature*. Winnipeg: Pemmican, (1889) 1992.

Greenblatt, Stephen. *Renaissance Self-Fashioning: From More to Shakespeare*. Chicago: University of Chicago Press, 1980.

Griffin, John Howard. *Black Like Me*. New York: New American Library, 1960.

Handy, W.C. *The Father of the Blues: An Autobiography*. New York: Macmillan. 1941.

Hardy, Campbell. *Sporting Adventures in the New World: Or Days and Nights of Moose Hunting in the Pine Forests of Acadia*. 2 Vols. London: Hurst and Blacket, 1855.

Harlow, Barbara. *Resistance Literature*. New York: Methuen, 1987.

Healy, J.J. *The Treatment of the Aborigine in Australian Literature*. St. Lucia: University of Queensland Press, 1978.

Heise, Ursula K. *Chronoschisms: Time, Narrative and Postmodernism*. Cambridge: Cambridge University Press, 1997.

Hindess, Barry. *Discourses of Power: From Hobbes to Foucault*. Oxford: Blackwell, 1996.

Hooks, Bell. *Talking Back: Thinking Feminist. Thinking Black*. Toronto: Between the Lines, 1988.

_____. *Black Looks: Race and Representation*. Toronto: Between the Lines, 1922.

Howard W. Odum and Guy B. Johnson. *Negro Workaday Songs*. Chapel Hill: The University of North Carolina Press, 1926.

Hubel, Teresa. *Whose India? Bakhtin and his World*. London: Routledge, 1994.

Hutcheon, Linda. *The Canadian Postmodern: A Study of Contemporary*

English-Canadian Fiction. Toronto, New York: Oxford U P, 1998.

Hyland, Peter. *Discharging the Canon*. Singapore: Singapore University Press, 1986.

Ihimaera, Witi and D.S. Long, ed., *Into the World of Light: An Anthology of Maori Writings*. Auckland: Heinemann, 1982.

Ilaiah, Kancha. *Why I am Not a Hindu: A Sudra Critique of Hindutva Philosophy, Culture and Political Economy*. New Delhi: Samya, 1999.

Itwaru, Harichand Arnold. *The Invention of Canada*. Toronto: TSAR, 1990.

Jaine, Linda and Drew Hayden Taylor. *Voices: Being Native in Canada*. Saskatchewan: University of Saskatchewan, 1995.

Jameson, Fredric. *The Political Unconscious Narrative as a Symbolic Act*. London: Routledge, 1993.

John W. Work. *American Negro Songs*. New York: Howell, Soskin, 1949.

Jones, Leroi. *Black Music*. New York: Morrow, 1967.

Jordan, Glenn and Chris Weedon. *Cultural Politics: Class, Gender, Race and the Postmodern World*. Oxford: Blackwell, 1995.

Keen, Ian, ed. *Being Black: Aboriginal Cultures in 'Settled' Australia*. Canberra: Aboriginal Studies Press, 1994.

King, Bruce, ed. *New National and Post-Colonial Literatures: An Introduction*. Oxford: Clarendon Press, 1998.

Keeshing-Tobias, Lenore. 'Stop Stealing Native Stories,' *Globe & Mail*, Jan. 26, 1990. 7.

King, Thomas, Cheryl Claver and Helen Hoy, ed. *The Native in Literature*. Toronto: ECW Press, 1987.

King, Thomas, ed. *All My Relations: An Anthology of Contemporary Canadian Fiction*. Toronto: McClelland and Stewart, 1990.

_____, ed. *An Anthology of Canadian Native Fiction*. Special issue of *Canadian Fiction Magazine* 60 (1987).

_____. *Medicine River*. Toronto: Penguin Canada, 1987.

_____. *One Good Story, that One*. Toronto: Harper Collins, 1991.

Klinck, Carl F. *Tecumseh: Fact and Fiction in Essay Records*. Englewood Cliffs, New Jersey: Prentice Hall, 1961.

Krupat, Arnold. 'Introduction.' *New Voices in Native American Literary Criticism*, ed. Arnold Krupat. Washington: Smithsonian Institution Press,1933.

_____. *Ethno Criticism: Ethnography, History, Literature*. Berkeley: U of California P, 1992.

_____. *For Those Who Came After: A Study of Native American Autobiography*. Berkeley: U of California p, 1985.

_____. *The Voice in the Margin, Native American Literature and Canon*. Berkley: University of California Press, 1989.

Kudchedkar, Shirin and Jameela Begum A. *Canadian Voices*. Delhi: Pencraft International, 1996.

LaRocque, Emma. *Writing the Circle: Native Women of Western Canada*, ed. Jeanne and Sylvia Vance. Edmonton. NeWest, 1990.

_____. *Defeathering the Indian*. The Book Society of Canada, 1975.

Lincoln, Kenneth. *Native American Renaissance*. Berkeley: University of California Press, 1983.

Loomba, Ania and Suvir Kaul. 'Introduction: Location, Culture, Postcoloniality.' *Oxford Literary Review: Writing History, Culture, Postcoloniality*, 3-30, 1994.

Lutz, Hartmut. 'The Circle as Philosophical and Structural Concept in Native American Fiction Today,' *Native American Literature*. Pisa, Italy: Servizio Editorial Universitario, 1989. 85-99.

_____. *Contemporary Challenges: Conversations with Canadian Native Authors*. Saskatoon: Firth House Publishers, 1991.

Machery, Pierre. *A Theory of Literary Production*, trans. G. Wall. London: Routledge, 1978.

Mannoni, O. *Prospero and Caliban: The Psychology of Colonization*. New York: Praeger, 1964.

Malouf, David. *Blood Relations*. Sydney: Currency, 1987.

Manuel, George and M. Poslns. *The Fourth World: An Indian Reality*. Toronto: Collier-Macmillan, 1974.

Maracle, Lee. *I Am Woman*. North Vancouver: Write-on Press, 1988.

_____. *I am Woman: A Native Perspective on Sociology and Feminism*. Press Gang, 1996.

_____. *Bobbi Lee: Indian Rebel*. 1975 (revised 1990).

_____. *Oratory: Coming to Theory*. 1990.

McLeod, John. *Beginning Postcolonialism*. New York: Manchester University Press, 2000.

Memmi, Albert. *The Colonizer and the Colonised*. New York: Orion

Press,1965.

Mohanty, Satya P. *Literary Theory and the Claims of History: Post-modernism, Objectivity, Multicultural Politics*. New Delhi: Oxford P, 1998.

Momaday, N. Scott. 'The Man Made of Words.' *Indian Voices: The First Convocation of American Indian Scholars*. San Francisco: The Indian Historian Press, 1970: 49-62.

Mongia, Padmini. *Contemporary Postcolonial Theory*. London: Routledge, 1998.

Monkman, Leslie. *A Native Heritage: Images of the Indian in English Canadian Literature*. Toronto: University of Toronto Press, 1981.

Morgan, Robin. *Sisterhood is Global: The International Women's Movement Anthology*. Garden City, NY: Anchor Books, 1984.

Morrison, R. Bruce and C. Roderick Wilson, ed. *Native Peoples: The Canadian Experience*. Toronto: Toronto UP, 1992.

Moses, Daniel David and Terry Goldie. *An Anthology of Canadian Native Literature in English*. Toronto: Toronto UP, 1992.

Muckle, Robert J. *The First Nations of British Columbia: An Anthropological Survey*. Vancouver: VBC Press, 1999.

Mudrooroo. *Indigenous Literature of Australia: Milli Milli Wangka*. Melbourne: Hyland House, 1997.

Naipaul, V.S. *India: A Wounded Civilization*. London: Deutsch, 1977.

New, W.H. *Native Writers and Canadian Writing: Canadian Literature*. Vancouver: UBC Press, 1990.

_____. *Borderlands: How We Talk About Canada*. Vancouver: VBC Press, 1998.

Newman, Peter. *Company of Adventurers*. Ontario: Penguin Canada, 1985.

Oliver, Paul. *Blues Fell This Morning*. London: Cassell, 1960.

Omvedt, Gail. *We Will Smash This Prison: Indian Women in Struggle*. London: Orient Longman, 1980.

Orbell, Margaret, ed. *Contemporary Maori Writing*. Wellington: A.H. & A.W. Reed, 1970.

Owens, Louis. *Other Destinies: Understanding the American Indian Novel*. Norman: U of Oklahoma P, 1992.

Parry, Benita. 'Resistance Theory/ Theorizing Resistance of Cheers of Natives,' *Colonial Discourse/ Postcolonial Theory*, ed. F. Barker,

P. Hulme and M. Iverson. Manchester: Manchester UP, 1994.

Paula, M.L. Moya and Michael R. Hames Garcia, ed. *Reclaiming Identity: Realist Theory and the Predicament of Postmodernism*. Orient Longman. India. 2001.

Petrone, Penny. *Native Literature in Canada: From the Oral Tradition to the Present*. Toronto: OUP, 1990.

Pollock, Griselda. *Vision and Difference: Feminity, Feminism and the Histories of Art*. London: Routledge, 1988.

Pollock, Sharon. 'Generations.' *Blood Relations and Other Plays*. Edmonton: Newest, 1981, 101-78.

Propp, Vladimir. *Theory and History of Folklore*, trans. Adiadn Y. Martin. Manchester: Manchester University Press, 1984.

Raja Sekhar, Patteti. *Discursive Displacement: The Jewish Canadian Discourse in Perspective*. Hyderabad: Navodaya, 2000.

Reid, Jennifer. *Myth, Symbol and Colonial Encounter: British and Mi' K maq in cadia, 1700-1862*. Ottawa: Univ. of Ottawa Press, 1995.

Rivikin, Julie and Michael Ryan, ed. *Literary Theory: An Anthology*. Oxford: Blackwell, 1998.

Ruoff, A. La Vonne Brown. *American Indian Literatures: An Introduction, Bibliography Review and Selected Bibliography*. New York: The Modern Language Association of America, 1990.

Rutherford, Anna. *From Commonwealth to Postcolonial*. Sydney: Dangaroo Press, 1992.

Ryan, Michael. *Marxism and Deconstruction*. Baltimore: John Hopkins, University Press, 1982.

Said, Edward W. *The World, the Text and the Critic*. London: Vintage, 1983.

_____. *Orientalism*. London: Penguin, 1978.

_____. *Culture and Imperialism*. London: Chatto Windus, 1993.

Sangari, Kumkum and Sudesh Vaid, ed. *Recasting Women: Essays in Colonial History*. New Delhi: Kali for Women, 1989.

Saraswathi, Pandita Ramabai. *The High-Caste Hindu Woman*. 1887. New Delhi: Inter-India Publication, 1984.

Sartre, Jean-Paul. *What is Literature?* Trans. Bernard Frechtman. London. Methuen, 1978.

Schafer, D. Paul. *Culture and Politics in Canada: Towards a Culture for All Canadians*. Markham: World Culture Project, 1998.

Sears, Djanet. *Afrika Solo*. Toronto: Sister Vision, 1990.

Selden, Raman. *A Reader's Guide to Contemporary Literary Theory*. Hertfordshire: Harvester Wheatsheaf, 1989.

Sharma, B.D. *Dalits Betrayed.* New Delhi: Har-Anand, 1994.

Shields, Carol. *Swan: A Literary Mystery*. Toronto: St. Oddart, 1987.

Shoemaker, Adam. 'Paper Tracks: Indigenous Literatures in Canada, Australia and New Zealand,' *New National and Postcolonial Literature: An Introduction*. Bruce King, ed. Oxford: Clarendon Press, 1998.

Smith, Sidonie and Julia Watson, ed. *Decolonizing the Subject: The Politics of Gender in Women's Autobiography*. Minneapolis: University of Minnesota Press, 1992.

Sommer, Doris. 'Not Just a Personel Story': Women's Testimonies and the Plural Self,' in Smith and Watson, ed. *De-Colonizing the Subject: The Politics of Gender in Women's Autobiography*.

Thiong'o, Ngugi wa. *Writers in Politics*. London: Heinemann Educational Books, 1981.

Spivak Gayatri Chakravorty. *In Other Worlds: Essays in Cultural Politics*. London: Routledge, 1987.

_____ . *Outside in the Teaching Machine*. London: Routledge, 1993.

_____. 'Subaltern Studies: Deconstructing Historiography,' ed. Ranajit Guha. *Subaltern Studies IV: Writings on South Asian History and Society*. Delhi: Oxford University Press, 1996.

Stein, Agnes. *The Uses of Poetry*. New York: Holt, Rinehart & Winston, 1975.

Sutherland, Ronald. *Second Image: Comparative Studies in Quebec/ Canadian Literature*. Toronto: New Press, 1971.

Swann, Brian and Arnold Kurpat, ed. *Recovering the Word: Essays on Native American Literature*. Berkeley: University of California Press, 1987.

Todoror, Tzretan. *The Conquest of America; The Question of the Other*. 1974. Trans. Richard Howard. New York: Harper and Row, 1982.

Troye, William ed. *The Oxford Companion to Canadian Literature*. Toronto: Toronto University Press, 1983.

Trigger, Bruce. *Go Natives and Newcomers: Canada's "Heroic Age" Reconsidered*. Montreal: Mc Gill-Queen's University Press, 1985.

Trevor, James. *English Literature from the Third World*. Beirut: Longman, 1986.

Tripathy, Rebati Bhallav. *Dalits: A Sub-Human Society*. New Delhi: Ashish, 1994.

Vizenor, Gerald. *Dead Voices: Natural Agonies in the New World.* Norman: U of Oklahoma P, 1992.

Welch, James. *The Death of Jim Loney*. Markharn, Ontario: Penguin Canada, 1987.

Williams, Raymond. *Marxism and Literature*. Oxford U. Press, 1977.

Woodcock, George. 'Prairie Writers and the Metis: Ruby Wiebe and Margaret Laurence.' *Northern Spring*. Canada: D.W. Friesen, 1987.

Woods, Tim. *Beginning Postmodernism*. Manchester: Manchester University Press, 1999.

York, Geoffrey. *The Dispossessed.* London: Vintage U.K., 1990.

Young, Robert. *Colonial Desire: Hybridity in Theory, Culture and Race*. London: Routledge, 1995.

_____. *White Mythologies: Writing History and the West*. London: Routledge, 1990.

Zelliot, Eleanor. *From Untouchable to Dalit: Essays on the Ambedkar Movement*. New Delhi: Manohar, 1998.